Dean

THE Times OF OUR Lives

The Times OF OUR Lives

RECOLLECTIONS FROM TOWN AND COUNTRY

Walter Love

Appletree Press

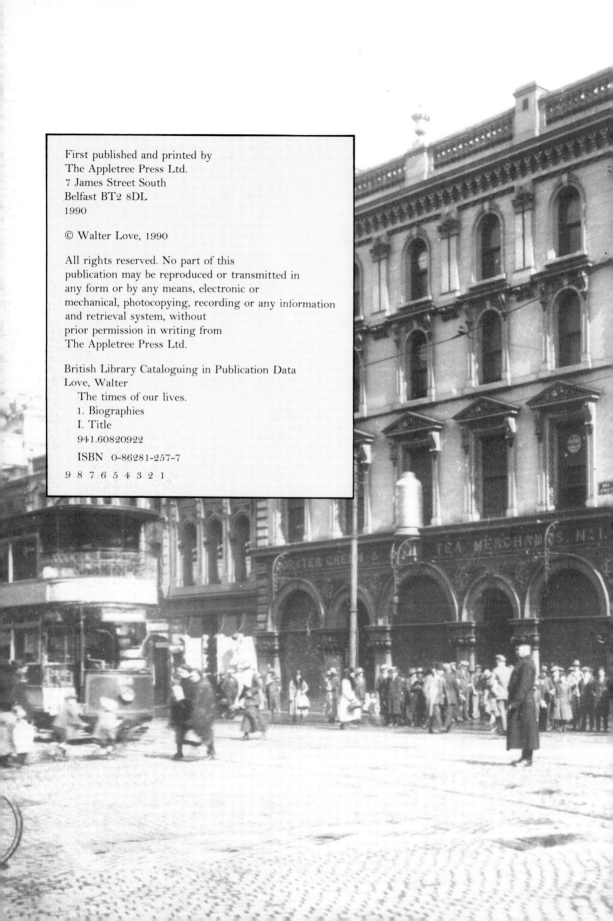

First published and printed by
The Appletree Press Ltd.
7 James Street South
Belfast BT2 8DL
1990

British Library Cataloguing in Publication Data
Love, Walter
    The times of our lives.
    1. Biographies
    I. Title
    941.60820922
    ISBN 0-86281-257-7
9 8 7 6 5 4 3 2 1

Contents

Preface

Conversation is of necessity a two-way business. Over the years as a broadcaster it has been my pleasure to meet and talk to people from all walks of life throughout the length and breadth of our Province. Perhaps I should say talk with, rather than talk to, because conversation involves listening as well as speaking.

In the past year or so I've been meeting and listening to many people, ordinary people, who've had something to say about themselves and their lives. And, especially, when they've talked about the way things used to be I've invariably found their stories to be fascinating.

Within the scope of a radio programme like BBC Radio Ulster's *Love Forty*, there are inevitably constraints on time. So for this book I've gone back to meet some of my guests again, to find out more about them and to share more of their experiences.

In saying that these are 'ordinary' people , I believe I'm paying them the compliment of acknowledging that they are all people who have lived their own lives, in their own way and, until now, well away from the spotlight: Michael McCullough became a carter for the carrying firm Wordie and Company at the age of thirteen and relates his life in Belfast before the chaos of the motor-car; Willie Grey, a Fermanagh man and 'local character' recounts tales of the Lough Erne area and its people; and Tom O'Kane, a man of indeterminate age, whose family has run the O'Cahan Arms in the village of Drumquin for several generations, tells of poteen-making and murder in the Tyrone countryside.

These and the other stories told here come from all parts of the Province, from city and town, village and countryside. While they are personal, I believe that taken together, and accompanied as they are by a wide range of contemporary and, in many cases previously unpublished photographs, they are marvellously evocative of a world and a way of life that may have passed but is clearly not forgotten.

Acknowledgments

I would like to express my gratitude to the subjects of the chapters of this book who talked to me with great enthusiasm about their lives and times. They also provided me with personal photographs which added greatly to what they had to say.

Others provided valuable assistance and helped me track down some excellent photographic material and to them also I am deeply indebted. The cover photograph of Hilltown Fair was taken by Ben Corr who sadly died in June this year. Ben had a deep love for the Ulster countryside and its people, especially in the Kingdom of Mourne. The many excellent photographs he took are a fitting memorial to him. I am grateful to his sister, Mrs Mabel McCrink, for permission to use some of his work.

Mr John Toner of Federal Express, successors to the firm of Wordie and Company, provided many of the illustrations which accompany Michael McCullough's text; Mr David Bigger and Mr Terry McDonald kindly allowed me to use a number of photographs of Londonderry in times gone by. Thanks as well are due to the RUC Museum; the National Trust; Belfast Central Mission; The Public Record Office, for permission to use photographs from the Cooper Collection; The Trustees of the Ulster Museum; and Mr Ken Anderson of the Ulster Folk and Transport Museum. Photographs are included from several major collections – the Hogg Collection in the Ulster Museum, and from the photographic archives of the Ulster Folk and Transport Museum.

Michael McCullough

Dip, Pash and the Barking Dog

When I've gone to meet someone interesting it has, quite often, led to an introduction to others with a story to tell. That's how I first met Michael McCullough, a man who got to know the streets of Belfast perhaps better than anyone. And he did it at a more leisurely pace than is possible in the traffic-choked streets of today. It was probably inevitable that he would one day become a carter for Wordie and Company, whose horse-drawn carts were once a familiar sight on the streets of the city.

'I WAS born in John Street, just across from Wordie's front gate, and me da before me was one of their top drivers.'

In those days, between the two wars, Wordies was the biggest carrying firm in Belfast. In fact in every town in the

Michael McCullough

Province where there was a railway station, there was also a depot belonging to Wordies. Horsepower meant something different at that time, and Michael learnt the necessary skills early in life.

A little before Michael McCullough's time perhaps, but these substantial premises in Corporation Street, Belfast, show the important position which Wordie and Company held in the days when horse-power predominated. Lined up here are some of the firm's four-wheeled vans, with a float (second in line) which was used to carry large panes of glass.

11

'For nearly a year they gave me a sort of a job driving the manager, Mr Alec Monro, around the town in his private gig. I can't remember now for sure, but with jobs hard to get maybe it was because I took a bit of care with my appearance that he used me. Maybe it was the bow tie and stiff collar.'

Maybe so, though even young Michael at the age of 13 couldn't match Mr Monro for elegance.

'He was a very dapper sort of a man. And there was never a morning he didn't have a rose in his buttonhole, fresh every day. He was known to be a very stern wee Scotsman, steadfast in his working rules and the like.'

Michael learnt to be punctual. At half past nine every morning he met Mr Monro outside the firm's Waring Street offices with the maroon coloured gig.

'It had to be looking its best, and every afternoon when I had put Rosie, the mare, to bed, I spent a couple of hours getting out the elbow-grease, cleaning the coachwork and putting a shine on the chrome ornaments on the patent leather harness. In the morning, with a curry comb in one hand and a brush in the other, I had Rosie looking her best too.'

But the hard work paid off because Mr Monro always had a good look at the gig to see that it was just right. Then they were off, the boss sitting beside Michael, a tiger-skin rug across his knees.

'It was a delight to drive with Rosie. You just had to take hold of the reins and steer her. She hardly needed me at all and could have found her own way to Wordies Divis Street yard.

'Traffic was very different then. Not too many cars about, a few solid-tyred lorries, but mostly carts. With so many mills and factories, like Coombe Barbour's, Mackies, the flour mills and the flax-mills, there was a constant stream of horse-drawn traffic up and down roads like the Falls. And I remember the funeral horses too. Lovely Belgian animals they were, mostly black with long tails. There was an old joke about people dying for a ride behind one of them. All horses had rubber pads between shoe and hoof, but those funeral horses must have been very lightly shod because you could hardly hear their hooves on the road.'

Only once did Michael feel the weight of Mr Monro's anger. He was to collect him from his house at Knock and take him to the early train to Dublin.

'I was supposed to pick him up at seven o'clock, but slept in. When I got to the stables in Divis Street the yardman, another Scotsman called Jimmy Sellars, was waiting with Rosie already harnessed. He was leaping up and down with anger. "Oh ye bugger o'Hiel," he shouted at me, in his acid Scottish tongue, and I don't know who was more frightened, Rosie or me, but she was almost jumping out of her skin. By the time I got near to Knockdene Park Mr Monro was out on the main road looking for me.

'God help you if I don't catch that train," was all he said to me, and then he struck Rosie with the whip, something I'd never seen him do before. She took off down the road so fast I could hardly hold her. If something had run out in front of us we'd never have stopped. We made it to Great Victoria Street station with seven minutes in hand, but poor old Rosie was steaming, and there was froth everywhere the harness touched.

'Before Mr Monro went into the station he glared at me. "If there's a hair out of place you needn't report here to pick me up tomorrow."

'I made sure there wasn't. I spent a long time that day rubbing her down with straw. I brushed her, dried her off and combed her tail and mane. When I met him the next day he gave her a good looking over, and no more was said about it.'

Twice a week Michael and Rosie had an extra job to do.

'Mr Monro had once lived on the other side of the city, somewhere off the Antrim Road. Every Tuesday and Friday, when we'd done the usual morning run, I was given a shilling to buy a packet of oatcakes from Maguire's Home Bakery on the Antrim Road. He must have been a customer of theirs when he lived there. Those oatcakes were then driven all the way across to Knock and delivered to his home. I suppose he thought the exercise would do us both good.'

Michael's chauffeuring ended within a year when Mr Monro's son bought his first motor-car.

'That put paid to me with Wordies for a while. My da had been with them for years and I can still remember watching him handle the company's show horses up at Balmoral. He was also a Union man, a shop steward with the Transport and General Workers.

'And, you know, that's why he got me the sack later on. I was helping one of the drivers who'd been given a new horse up from the country. Some of these horses could panic at the noises of trams and the like, and I was holding this horse's head steady while the driver was making a delivery outside the Grand Central Hotel in Royal Avenue. Along comes my da, sees me and says, "What the hell are you doin' there?"

'"Jock Stevenson sent me out to hold this horse for Willie John McNeice here."

'"Take the bloody horse home," he shouts at Willie John; "I'll not have him do a man out of a job."'

Even before he was in his teens, Michael had been on the lookout for work. When he was about 11 years old he was earning four shillings a week collecting newsreel films from the old Panopticon Cinema in High Street and delivering them to other city cinemas.

'Whenever a film, like the old Pathe Pictorials, had been shown in the Panopticon I re-wound it and took it to the New York Cinema in York Street. When they had shown it I re-wound it again and took it over to the Queen's in York Road, and then up to the Lyceum on the Antrim Road, on the corner of New Lodge and Halliday's Road.

'Having walked all the way up I took the tram back down into town. Mr Stewart, who ran the Panopticon, paid me my money, and if I wanted to go to any of the other picture houses in town I could get in free by telling them I worked for him.

'I tried all sorts of jobs back then, whatever came around. There was a boys' 'buroo' in the old Grand Central, so I signed on and was lucky enough to get a card to go for a job at a grocer's shop, Dornan's at 155a Antrim Road. As I didn't even have the money for the tram, I started to walk there. Somewhere along the way a lorry stopped beside me and I jumped up on the back. There were two others doing the same thing and I was passing the time of day with them.

'"How are ye doin'," says one. "Where are you goin'?"

'I replied, "I'm goin' up to Dornan's on the Antrim Road for a job."

'Without another word they heaped me off, and it was only when I got to Dornan's that I realised why. They were after the same job.'

But Michael had more success than they had, and when Mr Dornan found that he could read, write, count and handle a horse, the job was his. Two ponies were used for deliveries to all parts of the city and beyond. Some of those delivery runs took most of the day.

'I could find myself setting out from the Antrim Road to deliver to the top of the Lisburn Road. Then back down to Stranmillis, across to the Ormeau Road, over to Madrid Street off the Albertbridge Road, and then all the way out along the Old Dundonald Road as far as Ballybeen.'

This was in the early twenties and, in yet another of the periodic cycles of violence Belfast is prone to, a curfew had been imposed from 10.30 p.m. With such long delivery runs Michael was well after curfew many a night.

'Last thing I had to do was stable the pony and then make my way back on foot to Albert Street where we lived then. There was a real risk of being shot, but the nearest barracks at Cullingtree

The Grand Central Hotel in Royal Avenue, for many years Belfast's top address. Michael McCullough knew the exterior better than the interior, apart from his attendance at the boys' 'buroo' when jobs for young men were hard to find.

In 1935 most routes across the Irish Sea began at Donegall Quay in Belfast and it was a busy place every evening with the passenger boats waiting to leave for Ardrossan, Glasgow, Heysham and Liverpool. In the foreground is the old wooden jetty used by the Bangor boat.

Road was close to home and I knew all the policemen by name. I never had any bother though often enough I was told to "Get away home out of that."

'Because of unemployment I might have ended up in Canada at one time. They were training young fellas like myself for farming jobs in either Canada or Australia. I went on a training course at Richill Castle in County Armagh where they even gave us Canadian farm machinery to practice on. But then we were told that unemployment was just as bad over there and the thing was scrapped.

'One time I applied for a job with a printing firm in the city. They were looking for a young fella' to deliver paper on one of those old heavy delivery bicycles. But I was turned down, and I think it was because of the school that I went to. That's the way it was then. I met the boss years later, and did him a favour. He was badly stuck for an urgent delivery of paper. It was during the July holidays and I carried the supplies up for him. He wouldn't have been fit to carry them himself, they weighed so much. He rewarded me with £2 which was big money then, and said it was a pity there weren't more around like me. I told him that he had once turned me down for a job. He said nothing for a minute and then he apologised to me.'

Just before the Second World War Michael came back to Wordies.

'I began as a spellsman. The same sort of system operated in the docks. As a spellsman at Wordie's you had to stand over at the Christian Brothers School till you were called. But again, jobs were hard to get and you would have worked at anything. After four months you were made constant. To join the Carters' Union cost £2.10s. and I didn't have it, so I borrowed the money to get started.'

It was a tough life and in the early forties the carters went on strike 'looking for conditions'.

'If it was a tough life you didn't think about it that way. I was glad to have a job. On 57s.6d. a week I married my girlfriend Eileen on Boxing Day 1940. That was a pretty good wage then. The trouble was wages went flying in other places, but ours stayed much the same. Some places were paying six or seven pounds a week during the war and we were getting only half that. For going on strike we ended up being fined £5 and hardly saw any difference.'

A normal week for a carter was 48 hours though, with the war on, there was a lot of night-time working too. There were times when Michael got back home at 5.30 in the morning and still had to be back at the Heysham boat sheds on Donegall Quay by 8.00 a.m.

'The usual week was eight-and-a-half hours a day for five days, and we worked on Saturdays until 1.30 p.m. To make sure we did the full week they made us wait till that time on a Saturday before we got our pay.

'Although the day began at the Heysham boat at eight in the morning, and we didn't go on pay until then, we started work much earlier because first of all you had to collect the horses from Divis Street, have them brushed and the harnesses cleaned, and make your way with them down to the docks. And the same thing happened at night, off pay at the docks, and the horses to be taken back to Divis Street for the night in your own time.'

The stables were built to hold 68 horses, but because of lack of space, they had to be accommodated on the first and second floors of the building.

'The concrete ramps were very steep but had wooden straps across them to give the horses a footing. And you would throw peat down for them to make it easier. There was a forge and each horse had its hooves numbered. They kept sets of shoes ready made-up and your horse would be re-shoed at regular intervals. It only took about fifteen or twenty minutes to do this.'

Drivers were always exposed to the elements, winter and summer. Michael laughs when he thinks back to the days when the sleet and snow of winter beat down on him.

'Look at that. A good head of hair yet, and thank God I haven't an ache or pain in my body. Not bad for a man in his eighties.'

Underneath their carts the drivers kept a good supply of bale sheets. These were their wet weather gear. And when one got wet through, there was always another one.

'But the thing I liked best of all was the freedom. You were your own boss and you usually worked with the one horse so you got to know it and it got to know you. If the streets were slippy the horse would soon know if you were nervous. And tramlines could give you a bad time. You could topple a load because of them. Tarmacadam could be very slippy when it got wet, but even worse were the streets they paved with wooden sets. Even a shower of rain made them like ice.'

And there were plenty of wooden-paved streets in Belfast. They were used to cut down the noise of the carts outside all the main churches and outside important public buildings. Donegall Square was paved that way, as was Waring Street.

'Winters seemed to come earlier in those days. I can remember by November time the streets of Belfast would be iced over by the middle of the afternoon. We used to carry packets of 'cogs' with us which we hammered into the horses' shoes. These spikes gave them a better grip in winter but were hard to get in and out. And you had to take them out before the horses were bedded down or they'd have cut themselves to pieces with them.'

But if the tramlines could cause problems, they could also be useful at times. Michael remembers the steep hill on the Donegall Road at the old Windsor Cinema, where the road climbs up to the railway bridge.

'I used to wait at Rydalmere Street just off the main road until a tram went past. I knew that there'd be about ten minutes before there'd be another one, so I'd head out into the Donegall Road and get the wheels lined up in the tramlines, and away we'd go. We could sail up the hill as easy as anything.

'There's something else I remember about the Donegall Road when I had a horse called Jim. Jim liked his lemonade and whenever we had to call at the Irish Direct Trading Company's yard he wouldn't leave without a bottle or two. The foreman was an

obliging sort of an individual and used to hold the bottles up to the side of Jim's mouth. But the foreman didn't have to put up with what I did, because the lemonade always gave Jim a bad attack of the wind, and he blew musical fruit all the way back to town!'

Not only did the carters work longer hours during the war, but the range of goods they carried was much greater than in peacetime.

'There were the great bales of Air Force cloth lifted at the docks for Faulkner's Faulat Shirt Factory in Agnes Street. And when the air raids started the Anderson shelters came. Heavy sheets of steel came off the boats, and we had to carry them to wherever they were put together. But the heaviest of all were the metal castings we took empty to Coombe Barber's mill, and took back to the docks full, as artillery shells.

'I remember too the railway line which ran under the roadway at Queen's Bridge. Goods trains could get from the GNR round to Maysfield, past Oxford Street and the Central Yard and alongside the sheds on Donegall Quay. But if some of the wagons were too high and couldn't go through the tunnel, they had to be shunted into sidings and Wordie's men would unload them and take them down to the docks.

Coombe Barbours transformed metal castings into artillery shells during the Second World War. Cargoes like these, both inward and outward, were moved through the streets of Belfast by Wordie's men.

Mr Alec Monro never had to queue for the Dublin train at the GNR station in Great Victoria Street, but in days of austerity and food rationing north of the border thousands did, hoping to return undetected with something to add to the frugal diet of the years during and after the war.

'During the war we must have carried hundreds of thousands of eggs from the railway wagons. They were packed in big wooden cases filled with straw and sometimes if the wagons were shunted too hard there'd have been scrambled eggs everywhere.'

Many of Michael's workmates from those wartime days, and before, are gone now. But he still remembers the characters. 'Dip' Pennington got his name because they said he lived on dipped bread.

'There were the times he forgot to tie his loads on properly. There's a narrow wee street called Wellington Street that runs into Donegall Square. 'Dip' was collecting empty containers from the back of Hogg's china shop. He stacked the cart as high as he could and set off. But Wellington Street had a steep camber and he'd only gone a few feet when the whole lot swayed, hung for a moment, and toppled sideways. There was a barber's shop in the way and the people in it were trapped till they'd cleared up the mess.

'And 'Dip' always tried to blame his horse for everything. Like the time he took a load to the Great Northern Station in Great Victoria Street. When they told him it was for the Midland Railway in York Street, 'Dip' went up to the horse, looked it straight in the eye and shouted, "Ye stupid animal, ye've brought me to the wrong

Ann Street in 1946.

station." To teach it a lesson he bit it on the ear.'

Some of the horses had to put up with a lot, as could happen when the carters pulled a fast one on one of the boys.

'Johnny Galway used to mix water with his wine and drink it by the pint. When he called in to Phil Maguire's wine shop in Pilot

Ann Street, 1990.
Michael McCullough stands
where once horse-drawn vans
were common.

Street we knew he'd be there for some time. One day when Johnny came out of Maguire's he couldn't work out how the horse had got itself up on top of the cart, but there it was standing there with its head stuck in its nosebag.'

Sometimes it was the unsuspecting public who fell victim to the practical jokes of the carters. Michael recalls Pash Curley who was landed in court over one of his impersonations.

'Pash did a great imitation of a dog. He was sitting on his cart this day in Fountain Street when a smart-looking lady came round the corner from Wellington Place with an Irish wolf-hound on a lead. Pash jumped down and hid under the cart until she was about to pass, then out he sprang on all fours, barking his head off. The lady was so surprised she let go the lead, and the last was seen of the Irish wolf-hound it was going full pelt back round the corner and away up Wellington Place.

'Pash was made to appear in court for disorderly behaviour and when the magistrate heard about his impersonation of a dog he told him to show the court. Getting down on the floor, Pash did it again. It must have made a good impression because he was let off with a caution!'

Michael drove his cart through the streets of Belfast for over 17 years. But by the mid-fifties it was obvious that the days of the horse were numbered.

'I was among the last eight carters to work for Wordies and one of the few to make the changeover to the motor vans. I was lucky

Donegall Square South in 1946. Motor transport may have been taking over, but carters with their horses were still a familiar sight.

Jimmy Crossley posing beside one of the Scammell towing units which gradually replaced the horses. Michael eventually went on to drive one of the Scammells, and still remembers the inadequate lighting by today's standards; a single headlight and two sidelights.

too, because I had once had a motorbike, and had also learnt to drive a car.'

With that, and with his working knowledge of the streets of the city, Michael stayed with the firm as a driver.

'Mind you, I still missed my horse. There wasn't as much traffic then, but with the coming of the motor-van I was able to clock up a hundred deliveries in a day. I knew every shop in and around High Street, Ann Street and Cornmarket then. Names like Curleys, Sawers, Cochranes, and the big stores like Arnotts, Woolworths, Littlewoods, the Bank Buildings – and all of them. But several things were changing. As a carter I wasn't bothered much by the police. As a van driver it was different - you couldn't park here, you couldn't park there. But at least I could see things were getting fairer. Better pay, shorter hours, longer holidays.

'In the good old days I was often soaked to the skin. I was tired out at the end of a hard day, but I was usually very happy and when

I think back the thoughts are usually happy ones. It's still easy to hear again the clip-clop of the hooves of some of my four-footed friends of all those years ago.'

This group of Wordie's workers was photographed in the 1960s to mark foreman Billy McBride's retirement. Present were (left to right) Frank Craig, Hugo Malone, Peter Sullivan, (unidentified), Billy Smith, ex-Ireland international goal-keeper, Billy McBride, Tommy Tierney, Sammy Daley, Peter Kane (with youngster), Michael McCullough, Mickey Welsh and John Fox. The photograph was taken at Wordie's Falls Road depot. The corn loft is on the left in the background, and just visible on the extreme right, the ramp used by the horses leading to the stables at the rear.

Mick, Kitty & Bridie Matthews

The Cunning of the Mullaghmore Blackbird

Most people probably know the Mourne Mountains from the seaward side. The inspiration for Percy French's famous song was the sweep of the mountains as seen from afar. And the coastal road from Dundrum right round to the port of Newry gives prominence to the full height of the peaks as the land gives way to the sea.

But there is another side to the Mournes. As you travel south from Rathfriland to Hilltown and on through to the shores of Carlingford Lough at Rostrevor you cut across the mountains, and in some ways they seem less impressive, less dominating. Close above Hilltown, nestling against the aptly named Sheep Hill, lies the townland of Leitrim.

Mick Matthews was born here and still lives with his two sisters, Kitty and Bridie, on the family farm. The farmhouse itself goes back nearly two hundred years, but the family came here even further back. In the dark days of Cromwell's forays in Ireland, they moved to the Mourne country from Ardee in County Louth.

'BRIDGET McGuigan brought with her some thorn quicks from Ardee, and a bushel of flax seed. The hedge is growing there yet alongside the house. She married Patrick Matthews, and they had two sons, Patrick and Xavier. When she died she was waked for two days, and her remains taken by cart back to her birthplace at Ardee.'

According to Mick many of the customs and traditions of the area go back further than most people can remember. And some of the stories recall the days long before there was a police barracks in Hilltown, when the Revenue men had to travel on horseback all the way from County Antrim on the track of the smugglers, and the poteen-makers, who knew the area well.

'The Brandy Pad was the smugglers' route through the mountains. They'd have loaded up in Kilkeel off the boats and come up

the Pad to Hilltown and on to Newry or even as far as Dundalk. And I couldn't say for sure when the poteen started here. Some say it was two Danes, a father and son, introduced it to Ireland over 200 years ago. They started making poteen out of heather, but when the Revenue were near to taking them, the father shot the son and killed himself.'

Over the years there's been a continuing battle of wits between the authorities, originally the Revenue men - in more recent times the Customs and Excise and the police - and some of the great characters who have lived their lives trying to outwit them. Kitty retells a well-known incident which happened around the turn of the century.

'Turf used to be taken by the cartload from the bogs, like the Castle Bog which has been worked for hundreds of years. And the turf carts was a good way of moving poteen from one place to another, buried under a stacked cart. One day two men were taking a couple of cartloads of turf down to Newry. One cart was pulled

Mick Matthews looks on as Kitty hands Bridie turf for the fireside at their farmhouse at Leitrim in the Mournes.

27

Occasionally the police tracked down illicit stills, and were never slow to show off their captures. It is not recorded whether the police regarded the bottle as half full or half empty!

by a white horse and the other by a black one, and the Revenue had been tipped off that there was poteen concealed in the cart drawn by the white horse.

'But the turf cutters had been tipped off as well, so before they got to Newry they changed horses. When they got to the town police stopped them and bought the cartload drawn by the white horse. All they got for their trouble was a load of turf. The poteen continued on its way and disappeared without trace.

'There were two old men lived at Cabra, Arthur Fegan and Neil Woods. They knew all there was to know about poteen. Fegan was known as 'Stench' Fegan. I suppose that was because of the smell that came from the making of it. That and the smoke from the fires they lit meant that they worked their stills up in places like Shankey's Hollow on the Batt Estate. Neil Woods had a visit from the police one day, looking for stuff. But there wasn't a drop in his house. Constable Chatten even examined a row of glasses he found

on a shelf and gave them a good sniff. "You needn't be afeared, Constable," said Neil, "for I always wash me glasses. They're all clean."'

Local people paid ground-rent to Batt's Estate up to 1972, though land was sold off in 1912 and the mountain areas in 1915. Four townlands, Ballyaughian, Ballymaghery, Ballynanny, and Leitrim made up the Batt Estate, with 4,000 acres of mountain land. In earlier times farmers from a wide area drove their cattle up to summer pastures on Hen Mountain or Termonbrock. They'd have come from as far away as Lisburn, Lurgan and Banbridge. Mick remembers hearing about the way they lived their lives.

'They built Booley huts for themselves and their wives and families. These were round sod huts which they thatched with heather and rushes. They were built up to the last century and you'll find traces of them up on the mountain. Those were the days before they built the Mourne walls. The wives made their own butter which they put in small barrels called firkins, and they buried them in the moss over the summer to keep it cool. It came out the same as it went in the first day. And if they had bees they brought

Poteen-makers operated in the more remote areas where the smoke and the smell were less likely to be detected.

29

them with them to make heather honey. The heather honey would have been sold in some of the bigger towns like Rathfriland, Banbridge or Belfast.'

It was in July 1986 that the local newspaper, the *Outlook*, advertised 'the first annual Booley fair'. This was a very successful attempt by the community in and around Hilltown to recapture the atmosphere and the lifestyle of bygone days. So enthusiastically did some people embrace the idea that they did without electricity for the five days of the fair. No television for them. Instead the sound of old wind-up gramophones listened to by the light of oil lamps.

For younger people today the idea of making your own entertainment is seen as something highly unusual, but even for those whose memories don't go back all that far, it conjured up the atmosphere of the once popular ceilidhs. Many local farmhouses, like the Matthews' homestead, played host to thousands of neighbours over the years. Bridie Matthews shares her sister and brother's pleasure in recalling those days.

'There was always good crack round the fireside. Seven or eight neighbours might drop in of a night. Often it was just for a bit of conversation or to tell a yarn or two. Tommy Devlin was a great poet; in fact he was a genius. The late Peter Keenan was known as 'Dacency'. When he died, one of the locals was heard to say, "We've just buried the last bit of dacency in the place!"

'James Gilmore was a blind man who had a great memory. He could recall every verse he heard, and he was a frequent visitor. He lived about a mile away and always got himself home on his own along the road and up his own lane. Of course it didn't matter to him whether it was light or dark. One night another friend, Eddie McGinn, set off home in a thick mist and he got lost in a field. He had to call out for Oul' Gilmore to take him and lead him down to the road.'

It was on nights like that, that the stories would be told of the area and its people going back over the years, sometimes long before the times of those present. Like the story Kitty told me which she heard from another local character, Robert Trimble.

'A hundred or more years ago, Alec Heaney stopped at Johnston's early on a very hot summer morning. A short while earlier his mother had died, and had been buried in Ballymoney Cemetery at Kilcoo. He arrived at Johnston's and was passing the time of day with them. Someone said to him, "Will you come in for a cup of tea?"

'"I can't" he replied, "I've my mother with me."

'"Bring her in."

'"I can't," was the chilling reply, "for she's dead. She's on my barrow outside."

'So she was, and he continued on his way, the barrow bearing his mother's coffin which he had dug up from the grave, and which he was taking the eleven or twelve miles to Kilbroney Churchyard near Rostrevor. She was re-buried there, and he was eventually laid to rest there himself. In Kilbroney you can still see his massive ten-foot-high headstone. To this day no one knows why he made this macabre journey.'

The area round Hilltown has always been a great place for fairies and leprechauns. While some of the old superstitions have died out, many are still observed to avoid trouble.

'Nobody would touch a fairy thorn or a fairy fort. There's a nearby farm, just across the valley, which never flourished. The man who built it was warned that the site lay across a fairy path. He ignored good advice and suffered as a consequence. His wife had given birth to their first child, a girl, she was lying in her cradle one day. The woman knew that it was advisable for her to lay the fireside tongs across the cradle when she went out of the room.

Mick, Kitty and Bridie enjoying their own fireside on a rare occasion with no visitors present!

'But she didn't do it that day, and when she returned the baby looked very different. She never grew properly and fretted a lot from that time on. That girl died about 1920 while still very young.

'Matthew Brannigan, another well-known local character, had more than one encounter with the fairies. He felt their presence one night, and trying to avoid them got into a field and couldn't get out. He walked about till daybreak, by which time they'd gone.

'Then there is the superstition about red-haired women. If you should have the misfortune to be first-footed at New Year by a red-headed woman, then bad luck will remain with you for the rest of the year. And any farmer on his way to a fair knows that should he meet a red-haired woman on the way he'd be better turning back, for he'd have no luck in doing business that day. In the 1940s, James Matthews had a garage. One day he was asked by a lady with red hair for a lift to Belfast. He almost didn't get there because he had five punctures along the way.

'And if you came across someone with 'a covetous eye' it could be just as serious. A motorist from Hilltown had an equally bad journey to Dublin despite the fact that his car had new tyres. A local blacksmith chased a man out of his forge and wouldn't let him near it again after he caused the death of his magnificent pet rooster. The rooster would strut in and out of the forge and round the feet of the horses being shod. An old man cast his eye on it one day and said to the blacksmith, "That's a lovely rooster." The horse he was about to shoe lifted its hoof and brought it down on the rooster killing it on the spot.'

At the age of 14 or 15 Mick Matthews left school and was employed by an old woman called Mary Burns, 'filling carts with sand to build houses with. I got two shillings a day, for ten hours a day, six days a week. And in the evenings I worked on the farm for my father as well.

'Nobody had a tractor in those days and you started up at the Castle bog, about four miles up from Leitrim, at half past eight in the morning. That meant an early start to walk all the way up, with another walk down when you finished at seven in the evening. The turf was turned, footed and built out in a stack to season. It took a couple of weeks for them to dry out and lighten.

'That made it easier to load them on the cart to bring them down to the farmyard or garden. They were re-stacked there for the winter. About 25 or 30 cartloads would give a year's supply. After the turf was stacked it was time for the turnips and by July the hay would be ready for cutting. If you kept sheep, they would be clipped in July as well.

'And then, at the start of August, there was flax to be pulled.
That was slavish work, very heavy and laborious. It was put in the
dam to "ret" it, and had to be trampled down with your bare feet.'

This was work carried out by the women as well, and Kitty
remembers the horrible smell as the flax retted.

'It was worst at first, but after a time you didn't notice it as much.
After about ten nights it was taken out and thrown on the brew, or
brow, of the dam. This got the water out of it and let you take it
by horse and cart to the fields to spread out and dry out. But if the
weather wasn't good it blew about everywhere.

'When it was dry enough it was lifted again and tied up in
"beats". The last of the drying was done in "ricks" or "double stooks"
before it was taken to the mill for "scutching". Bleaching was done

*Extra helpers of any age are
always welcome when there's
work to be done.*

Flax carts at Rostrevor in 1941.

at Martin's Green at Rostrevor, and there was another green in the townland of Ballyaughian near Hen mountain – it was also known as Martin's Green. My father, John Matthews and other local farmers took flax to Tollerton's Mill, near Rostrevor, to have it scutched.'

The never-ending work of the farm continued month by month, with the harvest in September, potatoes in October and all the tidying up and cleaning out of 'sheughs' during the winter, ready for the cycle to begin again in springtime. Mick can recall a number of very severe winters in the Mournes.

'There were very heavy snowstorms in 1940, and in 1947 the snow lasted nearly eight weeks. The last bad one was in 1963. In the early years there were no mechanical diggers and the roads would be closed for weeks. If the snow lay and then froze during the night it was easier to walk on it. We could make a path and walk down to Hilltown. I can remember places along the road where there were drifts twenty-five feet high. The farmhouse is below the level of the hedge and I can remember people walking along level with the chimneys. With sheep out on the mountain we did our best to get hay to them, till the snow would thaw a bit and they could get down to a bit of heather. Many a time you would have had to dig some of them out. But we never lost too many of them; they usually survived if they weren't covered.'

Kitty and Bridie always kept a good supply of basic groceries to hand, especially in winter. When the local delivery vans had difficulty operating they would have had enough flour, wheatmeal and oatmeal, and their own butter and milk to keep going. Tea and sugar might have been a problem if the roads were closed for long. And, of course, on most farms they'd have kept a pig.

'We used to have a pig for our own use. It was fattened on potatoes and, especially, buttermilk and plenty of yellow meal. And when the man came along and killed the pig and put it in the salt, the taste of it was lovely. We had the bacon and pork steaks all winter. Lovely flavour!'

And Mick claims that the bacon of long ago, from your own pig, was a lot better than the bacon people buy today.

'If you were going by the road you could have told who had the bacon on. It was a great smell. It always reminds me of Sunday mornings.'

In their earlier days, Kitty recalls the 'home baking' and the cooking done by her mother.

'She had a very large griddle, because there were eight of us in the family at that time. In fact ten, counting both parents. So she had to bake four griddles of bread every day. And the old oven pots that you hung on the crook, she used to make lovely big apple cakes on them. But you had to make sure that you had turf, because any other fuel would be no good to heat the lid of the oven pot. That was the way to make apple cake and oaten cake as well.

'She kept a lot of turkeys coming up to Christmas, and when the turkeys were fat and ready to sell they were brought to the market in Rathfriland. The money that was made from the turkeys she took to Thompson's the drapers, and she bought all the clothes for us girls, and the boys for the springtime. Socks and jackets and jerseys and things for school. And she would also have got together all the ingredients for the Christmas cake and the pudding.

'To make her Christmas pudding she always used a very large bowl, and she never used a recipe. It was just a handful of this and a handful of that, currants, raisins and sultanas and all the mixed peel. Everything was put in a flour bag and it must have weighed about 14 lbs. She boiled it in a three-legged pot on the fire. And it was boiled for so long, and then it was taken off and put on a big, willow pattern side-dish.

A typical 'scutch' mill.

'She would have sprinkled it over with brandy and put a piece of holly on top of it. It was really delicious. And when we got tired eating it, she used to slice it up and fry it in the pan.'

The flour bag that Kitty's mother used to boil her Christmas pudding was one of many which were put to good use by farmers' wives.

'Flour bags were saved, and when she had a dozen or so of them, the lettering was removed and they were bleached and hung out on the hedgerow. Later the stitching would be removed and they were made up into sheets, bolster covers and pillow cases. Four made a sheet, two a long bolster, and one a pillow case.

'A bog bag was a flour bag used to carry food for the turf cutters up on the Castle bog. It would usually have been filled with soda bread, and oaten bread with home made butter, and tea and sugar.

'Joey Kelly from Kilcoo has for some years now had a van trailer which we christened 'Kelly's Canteen'. In it there are shelves and hooks for hanging up the tea mugs, and in bad weather it gives us a bit of shelter up on the bog.'

For the womenfolk, especially the daughters in the family, there was little let up in the daily routine. Kitty hated the drudgery of twisting straw into ropes, something she often used to do when she came home from school. Churning butter also required stamina, more so in winter with the lower temperatures, and on many a day there was no tea until the butter was made.

And the girls had no trouble sleeping at the end of days spent working with the potato crop.

'First we had to gather them, digging with spades. We only gathered the big ones, the small ones were left for feeding the pigs and hens. And the big ones had to be separated to get rid of any bad ones. But the worst part was bringing them to the heaps, or pits, to fill them in to keep them for the winter.

'In November, when it got dark on the shorter days we'd work by the light of hurricane lamps until all the potatoes were covered up. Now that was really hard work.'

In those days workers were taken on at the Hiring fairs in places like Newry and Castlewellan. Most of these workers desperately seeking employment for the following six months came from the South. A hundred years ago a ploughman would have earned £12 for six-months work. But a yardman or a servant girl would have earned only £8 or £9, depending on the house. 'There were some bad houses in them days, God help them.' Not only was it hard work, but very often the food was bad and for living accommodation the workers lay out in the barn over the cows. Being tough and healthy was a definite advantage.

The whole of the local farming community would descend on Hilltown for the monthly fairs held on the second Tuesday each month. Other local fairs were held in Warrenpoint, Rathfriland, Kilkeel and Castlewellan. Mick remembers them all.

'When you were driving the sheep or cattle down the road you'd often see the dealers coming up the road to meet you. They would offer you a price along the road and if you weren't sharp you'd find your own livestock on sale at much higher prices when they offered them for sale again in the market.'

As a young man Mick took horses on foot all the way to the Bann fair in Banbridge, or the horse fair in Camlough. If it meant a three- or four-hour walk, he'd be on the road by six in the morning.

'When I went with my father and the horse and cart to Newry with a load of potatoes, we'd be on our way at four in the morning, and maybe get sixpence a hundredweight for our trouble. But the greatest difficulty was with the animals. Some would bolt and run away. And on a winter morning, with so many steep hills around, an animal could have broken a leg if it slipped and fell. When that happened it had to be shot and that was a complete loss. Luckily, it never happened to one of my animals. Nobody liked to see Geordie Kelly from Newry coming. He collected dead animals, but they had no value to the person who owned them.'

In the days when there was very little in the way of organised entertainment in areas like the Mournes people created their own entertainments. At certain times of the year dances took place as a form of celebration. As well as harvest dances, there were flax-pulling dances. Kitty and Bridie may have found working with the flax hard going, but the dances were memorable.

'People came from far and near to the flax-pulling dances. They were held in barns and went on all night. Often the set dances were accompanied by a lilter, known as the "timer", who kept his foot going all the time. And what were called American wakes were held for anyone emigrating to America. These were big dances held in the home of the person who was leaving or in a neighbour's house.'

With no other entertainments, and certainly no public places to hold dances, the phenomenon of 'crossroads dancing' was a particularly strong one in the locality. These were held on Sunday evenings in the summertime, and attracted hundreds from the surrounding parishes. A popular venue was Biddy Doyle's corner in the townland of Ballyvally, and the musicians would probably have accompanied the dances with a mouth-organ, melodion or fiddle.

According to some sources, Biddy Doyle was quite a character.

In her shop she sold everything, and everything often included a drop of poteen.

When poteen was moved around the country from place to place for safe-keeping, some of the local ballad singers passed on information at the ceilidhs by including references to local places in the words of the songs they sang. 'The Blackbird's Sittin' Clockin' in the Hills of Mullaghmore' was a song often used in this way.

In 1923 Canon Rooney, the parish priest at Clonduff, opened a parochial hall, and the dances continued indoors from then on. From that time, crossroads dancing gradually disappeared. The parochial hall dances charged a shilling to get in, and often there were many more outside the hall who hadn't the money to get in.

Money wasn't all that plentiful for many of the folk of Leitrim. Times were often hard, but most of the memories they enjoy sharing today are happy ones, times when the 'crack' was good.

Cross-roads dancing was a very popular tradition in the Mournes and for many was their only entertainment. The practice died out shortly after this rare picture was taken in the late 1920s when the church provided halls for local entertainments.

OPPOSITE:
Ben Corr worked for the old Ministry of Agriculture in the Mourne country for many years. He often took his camera with him for his own pleasure and to provide a record of the people of the area. This magnificent portrait of cattle dealers resting at Hilltown Fair in 1959 shows his considerable talent to good advantage.

41

Tom O'Kane

Three Halves Without a Measure

Several years ago I came across a small booklet about the Tyrone village of Drumquin. It was produced by the village Youth Centre's committee and was their third such venture. One of their aims was to raise the quality of life in their community, and at the same time to raise funds for the young people of the area.

One chapter in particular attracted my attention. It was the story of a celebrated local hostelry and of the family who have run it for several generations. Head of the family is Tom O'Kane, a man who is either in his late eighties or early nineties, depending on who you talk to!

Drumquin lies surrounded by the green hills of Tyrone along the road from Omagh to Castlederg, and Tom O'Kane probably owes his longevity to the quality of life enjoyed by the inhabitants of this quiet backwater. He may have retired 'nominally' many years ago, but each time I've called in to see him, and to share his memories of the Drumquin of the past, I've found him behind the bar of the O'Cahan Arms, proud of the many generations who have served the public over the years.

'I CAN go back as far as my great-grandfather in these premises, but I couldn't tell you when the house was built. This side of the river is not really Drumquin at all, its Drumnaforbe, but since the building of the bridge over the river the whole place is known as Drumquin.'

Tom's memory is very clear, right back to the early years of this century. And he delights in recalling some of the great characters of the area.

'There was a lady, a pretty strong lady, she was about six foot and she used to shave every day, same as a man. She made poteen so the police was trying to get her on several occasions, both the Omagh police and the Drumquin police, but they failed to get her.

After a long time they went up to get her at Lough Bradan, where she was working the still. Well, they caught her redhanded, the still, the worm, the wash and everything else, including the poteen. So, of course, they took all to the barracks here in Drumquin. And they summonsed her and let her go to appear at Omagh Petty Sessions on the Monday morning.

'She didn't know what to do for she was caught openly. My Uncle William had a place at the foot of the town, and they had a sham battle on the Saturday night. They got a lot of boys, a lot of men, to have a fight and it got the police out. So the guard on the barracks, he was looking out the door at the battle going on, while she was round at the back of the barracks with a horse and a van. There was a big high wall, so she had this leather she put up on the wall and the help of a couple of men there with her.

'Well, she searched the place and she got the barrel, the still and the wash, and she got everything up in the barrel. She sat up on the wall and she got it all up on the leather and handed it over to the men. All the evidence she put on the van and that was that.

'Come Monday morning Molly was in the well of the court. The police had searched and searched the barracks and couldn't find a

Another successful police haul. Only in the case of Molly Mimee and her accomplices the evidence was recaptured from the police, lock, stock and barrel and as Tom O' Kane relates, 'No evidence, no case.' And the case against the famous Molly Mimee was dismissed.

thing. So the sergeant came into the court to explain to his Honour. He says, "We got the still and the barrel and everything else but we have lost it. We don't know where it went. It has been taken out of the barrack yard, and we don't know how they got it out." Well, his Honour says, "No evidence, no case", and he dismissed the case of Molly Mimee. So that was the famous Molly Mimee. Even now she is still talked about.

'She was a great woman for the English people coming over here for the shooting of the Grouse up on the mountain. She camped out with them. Alfie Woods was a great man about this town and we used to go for the fishing. We'd have camped out at Loughlea, about a mile-and-a-half over the mountain. It wasn't legal the way we were fishing. I was a lump of a lad about eight year old, and I'd a wee pool where the water'd go through but the fish weren't able to get out. Molly used to come with her bottle of poteen and two pints of milk, every night, and she stayed all night. She lay with me in a wee bed at the side of the river, and I always used to say I was the only one lay all night with Molly. She was a famous character.'

Tom tells me too that on occasions there were policemen up on the mountain at night, and others, playing the card game Nap all night, and no doubt up to all sorts of other activities as well. But at this distance the details are somewhat sketchy, and probably just as well! The first motor-cars appeared in Drumquin round about the start of the First World War, and here again young Tom came into contact with the law.

'Old Eddie Winters had a car, and Doctor Johnston over the bridge. Then we got a car, and came by two from America with left-hand steering. You had to swing them to get them started, there was no battery. There was a mag (magneto) on them and inside there was four coils, and you would see that you had four plugs sparking. And if there was no spark at one of the plugs you had to clean it and get it working.

'As fast as you could drive would be about 30 or 35 miles an hour. And that caused some commotion. They were running along the road holding horses, taking them up lanes and throwing bags over their heads when they heard the motors coming. And the roads isn't like now, of course. They were cut stone which had been levelled, and you would see the stones flying in all directions.

'The first time I got my licence I was a boy about ten. Well, I

45

went into Omagh and I saw a fella I knew, so I says to him, "I want you to go up to the court-house and say that you're Thomas O'Kane, of Main Street, Drumquin, and ask Mr Moffatt for a licence." He agreed to do it and I gave him the money, four shillings or something. No photo or nothing needed.

'Well, he came out with the licence and he gave it to me. So I was driving about, and I was in Omagh one day when I'd had the licence about a week. I was stopped in Bridge Street, opposite a man called Johnny McSorley - he was a bicycle man there. This policeman walked up and he looked at me and he walked up to the corner. He came down again and walked up again and then he spoke to me.

'"Who's the owner of this motor-car?"

'Says I, "I'm the owner."

'"Have you got a licence?"

'"I have". And I gave it to him.

'He took a good look at me because I had a big cap on me to make me look a bit older. And he says, "I'll hold on to the licence till we see about this." I got a letter the following morning anyway to tell me the licence was taken off me. But I got the last laugh on them.

'The County Inspector used to come out here, and he used to be in here with my father and Dr Johnston and Father Kelly and Andy Moffatt and all these people. They'd be drinking in the bar and, well, by the evening the County Inspector would be well lit. This night he turns and says, "Where's Tom, he'll take me into Omagh." I gets into the car, drives the County Inspector and the same said policeman was standing in Bridge Street when I went in. He saw the County and he saluted. The only thing I could think to do was to salute him back!

'So the County told me that he'd made arrangements that I could drive around Omagh and Drumquin with no bother or interference from anybody. So I was in with him every time, and that was all there was about it.'

Tom points out that all of this happened a long time ago in the days when you'd hardly meet another motor vehicle all day. But there were of course times when the main street of Drumquin was packed. On a Thursday, market-day, you couldn't move for people and their carts, and animals.

'We bought the house next door and there was a big iron outside, that was a weigh-bridge for the farmers with the carts and the pigs and the potatoes and the corn and everything. People came from all over the parish here, but the real big days were the Fair Days. The dealers came from Irvinestown, they came from Omagh, from Newtownstewart, from Castlederg and from all round. The cattle

was one of the big things on the Fair Days. We grazed about 150 head of cattle, all year olds, and I bought a lot of them. My father was ill at the time. I would have been about 14 or 15, and there were times I'd have had to buy three to get two because farmers with a couple of good cows would put them in the ring with one not so good as a lot of three. The price for 150 head of cattle was £750, a fiver a time. And after raising them for three months, I sold them at the August Fair out of the front of the door here. I sold 60 of them for £16 a piece, three times over their purchase price, and the rest at £14.'

Working from the front door had obvious advantages for the O'Kanes, and many a deal was completed over a glass or two in the bar. At one time there were many pubs in the village, though only one, Duncan's, in Drumquin proper, across the river. But with only a slight effort, Tom can list the rest of them.

'My Uncle William's was one, Donnelly's, Campbell's, Doyle's; there was an old inn in what is now McNulty's; Monaghan's at the corner, and ours; the O'Cahan Arms, making a grand total of eight. People didn't go short of a drink, and in my young day drink was very cheap.

'A half pint of whiskey would have cost you a shilling. And there was nobody interested in beers or stout. Do you know that when Guinness come here we couldn't even sell it! We couldn't give it

away, because it was the gypsies bought it. Nobody else would touch it. They were all whiskey drinkers. And do you know what made the difference? The Guinness went to the hospital in Omagh, and when the hospital got it, everybody drunk it afterwards.

'Every one of those pubs did a fairly good trade, because the people had no place else to go. Now in the change of times with the motor-cars it's all different. One night there I had three lads in the bar, and they were talking to me. I didn't know them at first, but I knew their fathers. Well, they had three bottles of beer, one each, and when they'd finished they wanted three more. But then one of

Not only have vehicles changed dramatically over the decades, road-making too used to be a simpler operation though it still involved large gangs of men.

them said, "No. No more. We're going down to the Border Inn to see who's in it." Now the Border Inn would be twelve or thirteen miles from here. So off they go and I expect they had a few drinks there, and then they'd have gone up to Castlederg afterwards. They change all around, that's the state of affairs with the cars.

'In the old days they had to stay. The town was packed on a Friday night, a Saturday night and, as I've said, on a Thursday too. They drunk in the rooms, they drunk out in the yard, they sat on the stairs or anywhere they could find if the bar couldn't hold them. The men were all whiskey drinkers until the stout come in, as I've said, and the women, when they come in in their shawls, they drunk gin. It was supposed to be good for the women in them days.'

With so much serious drinking going on, I was wondering if there was much drunkenness about.

'Not so much. An odd fellow on a Fair Day might have had too much to drink. My uncle was a magistrate; he was on the bench. When the police took a man in to the Barracks he would have appeared before my uncle. He would have dismissed all cases of drinking, and he often said, "When a man comes out for a day, well, let him enjoy his day. If he was just a few half-uns over the limit, well, that's all right. He's happy. Let him go home in his own ordinary way." Most of them weren't much harm to anyone else. They usually had to walk home anyway, or go by bicycle.'

And those were the days of the bona fide drinkers. The only customers legally entitled to a drink on a Sunday were bona fide travellers. These were defined by the law as anyone who had to travel at least three miles. This must have increased the traffic on the roads at weekends, though according to Tom they weren't all that sharp about it in the Drumquin area.

To allow some of his father's bar staff the day off on a Sunday, Tom started helping out while hardly able to see over the counter. At seven years old, he would have preferred to be outside playing football.

'I could hear the ball outside hoppin' around but I had to serve the people. And not only could I run a bar but later I learnt to break open the barrels of spirit and to blend the whiskey. The whiskey was sold to the publicans in barrels then, or in five-gallon jars. There were no travellers going round with a case of whiskey or a case of rum. The only whiskies you could get then was Powers and Jameson or Bush. And there was no beers of any kind, only Bass, and you had to bottle that too from the barrel. It had to stay for a fortnight for to settle, and once you turned it on for bottling you never could turn it off.

'You bottled it with one hand, and the other fellow put the corks in the bottles. Some of those bottles were made of crockery which meant you couldn't see into them. I think the Folk Park in Omagh have some of our old crockery bottles yet. When the glass bottles came in it was better for washing and seeing into them.

'But the whiskey was ordered by the barrel by my father and it would be delivered to us. It came to us pure clear, just like poteen. Well, you had to 'break' that whiskey and you had to get rain water,

An old label from the days when the O'Kanes blended and bottled their own whiskey.

spring water was no good to it. Rain water was a softer water and you had to mix it with that. Then you coloured it with stuff you got years ago from McAdams, the chemist in Omagh, or if you hadn't that you could burn some sugar and that did the job.

'Not only did you have to get the strength right, but you had all the government measures in the bar. We bottled it, labelled it with our own O'Kane's label, and capsuled it. And when I came to pour it I never used a measure. I used to take the bottle and go along and pour it, judging it by eye. There was a great argument one time with the Customs and Excise. This fellow was telling them that there was a man in Drumquin was a great expert without the measure. So they come in, three of them at the one time.

'He says, "Will you measure us three halves of whiskey without the measure?"

'Says I, "It's against the law, you know."

'And he says, "We're the Customs and Excise, and I was in here before when you were doing it. And these boys were saying you couldn't."

'Well, I agreed to do it and I put out my glasses and poured out three halves. And when they checked them they were dead on.

'He says, "Will you put out two more halves." I put them out, again dead on.

'"Well, God," he says, "that's wonderful."

'Of course, now with the changes in the glasses I wouldn't be as accurate, but with the old glasses I had for years and years I knew it.'

As far back as 1893 the Tyrone Directory shows several O'Kane enterprises among Drumquin's merchants and traders. These include family grocer, hardware, leather merchant, spirits' merchant and dealer in agricultural manures. Another side to the businesses run by Tom's immediate family was funeral undertaking.

'We kept about eight horses, and sometimes ten. Most of the horses for the hearse we would have bought at Ballinasloe Fair and we brought them up here. I trained them on the hearse but they could have done anything. We did the funerals for the workhouse in Omagh. We were paid thirty shillings for a coffin and a hearse to bring out the remains to the churches here. Now that's all I got for the funeral.

'There were different prices depending on what was wanted. For the top funeral, my coffin had panelled sides and mountings, everything on it. We put on the crucifix and breast plate and maybe a Sacred Heart badge down the front, and I got my bar mountings out of Germany. It was lined with pure silk and tassels over the coffin, three sets of them. With the hearse, a car or a coach to do the funeral and afterwards to leave the people home, my full account was £7. The cheap funeral was £4, and the workhouse funeral thirty shillings.

'My father was at one time on the Board of Guardians, and when the people had no money they would come for to see the Doctor. They would come into the bar and I would give them a line, a black line, and the doctor saw them for that. When they wanted to bring the doctor out to the house, they had to get a red line. And this was from the Board of Guardians in Omagh.

'I remember one time the hearse went in for a funeral of someone from the workhouse. And the man we got to take it often did this sort of job, Michael John McCanny. He was to take the remains to the chapel. He come along on a wild night with a terrible snow and everything else and he was half lit. He arrived at the house here for someone to give him a bit of a hand at the chapel. But when he looked into the hearse there was no coffin.

"'God," he says, "where's the coffin?"

'They turned the horses and they got a hurricane lamp and went back along the road. And there in a hollow at Unshinagh they found the coffin lying in the snow in the middle of the road. There was a board at the back of the hearse which must have slipped when a wheel went over a bump in the snow and the coffin slipped out. But they got it up to the chapel, and no one was any the wiser.'

Tom still has one of the old horse-drawn hearses and has no intention of getting rid of it. He was once offered over £2,000 for it which he refused. And in the bar are the set of lamps from it. In fact there are two sets of lamps in the bar: the smaller set was used on wedding carriages, and the larger one for funerals. An old saying

What the well-heeled motorist was driving around 1906. A Mr Hughes, possibly with his mother, at the wheel of his Darracq. French cars were popular for those who could afford them.

in the family runs, 'One set of lamps married them, and another set buried them.'

At one time the O'Kanes ran four or five cars, like jaunting cars, and these operated a passenger service into Omagh in the days before regular bus services.

'We ran a wagonette every Saturday which held 26 people, 13 on either side. It was pulled by two horses and it gave people most of the day in Omagh. Coming back, they were to be at the premises we kept at the top of Castle Street by about six o'clock in the evening, and all for a return fare of a shilling.

'Well, the wagonette would usually be packed up, and maybe horse and cars would go along with them too. It took inside an hour and a half to make the journey from Drumquin to Omagh, but with a good trotting horse you could do it in an hour.

'It could be a bit of a bumpy journey along the roads with the iron

hoops on the wheels, though later on we had a better one, a rubber wheeled car, which was smoother. The thing is, there was no roller for the roads at the time, and the way was for men to cut the stones, breaking them with a hammer into wee pieces. The roads was let out to local people to keep them, in them days, and some would have kept them well. But there were throughother people as well.

'And you had to pass the railway gates in Omagh there. A man by the name of Carson looked after them. He was a very odd old boy, you daren't move before your time. The train used to go up from Derry to Omagh, and my grandfather, James Woods of Connorbracken outside Omagh, he rode in the first train that ever

About ten years later, Mr Hughes, this time with wife and offspring, has progressed to another French make – a Clement-Bayard. Both cars bear the same registration number. An early form of Yuppyism perhaps?

55

left Omagh on his way to the markets. He was a pork-buyer for Biggars and for Sinclairs, and he used to do all the markets, Sixmilecross, Durragh and all these markets where the train went through. He never took a drink all the time he was in business until he come onto pensionable age, when he had to retire. And then he had a bottle of whiskey in every pocket until the day he died!

'Another relative of mine ran a band here and they used to go out for practice. Well one of them, Jimmy Gowan, he was a fluter and one night he was in the first line on the outside. So they gave the band their orders coming out of the yard to go up by the Manse, up at the top of the town, and to turn there and come down again. But they changed the orders, and he didn't hear the instruction to go round the corner first. So when the band went out and turned the corner, the boy walked on, him flutin' alone and when he looked around there was no sign of the band!'

As happened in so many small Ulster communities, there was a great deal of socialising between Catholic and Protestant neighbours.

'There was no such thing as what religion are you, or who are you or what are you. I went to the Orange Halls myself and danced, and my family along with me, and all the best of friends. The one would do anything for the other. They had a heart of corn all my early years and early days. I danced in Drumran Orange Hall and had a sister played the piano in it. We danced some nights until five o'clock in the morning. The dances now are over at two. They weren't over at two with us! It was five in the morning and clear daylight when we were comin' home.

'I remember one time my father was very strict on going out at night. That night we stole out, went out by the window. He never heard us so we went away to a dance. Well, when we got back - to make sure he never heard us comin' in - we went up to where the coffins was. And we pulled out two coffins and we got into one each and fell asleep. We had a great time in my younger days.'

But times have indeed changed and television is one of the factors which has brought about that change.

'They used to ceilidh years ago. That's when they used to sit round the fire and they would have a great night. So-and-so would be there and she'd make them a cup of tea, and if there was a law case about bog or a right of way it was fought with them around the fire. But now, from the change of times with the television, if you go now for to ceilidh, as they say, you go to the door. You rap and the wife comes out. "Keep quiet, keep quiet. Sit down there's somethin' on." And they play the television until twelve o'clock. You never get talking. You only get speaking at twelve o'clock when the television's all over, and then you get a cup of tea and go home and get no chattin' at all.'

Perhaps the most dramatic event with local connections which Tom can relate is of a celebrated murder in nearby Newtownstewart.

'Gordon Graham was manager of the Northern Bank in Newtownstewart in 1871. Every Thursday, being market day, he came to Drumquin to run the sub-office on the first floor of our premises. On the 29 June 1871, while he was here in Drumquin, his cashier, William Glass, was working in the branch office back in Newtownstewart. He had a pal, Inspector Montgomery of the RIC. Montgomery had got himself into difficulties about shares or something, and he went up at about five or ten minutes to three to the bank. He and the cashier were very great, so he was able to walk behind the bank counter. Now, he had a metal file in his hand, and he drove the file into the cashier's ear and killed him.

'He took all the money in the bank and he hid it at a place on the Omagh road called Grange Wood. Being a policeman himself, he was out with the rest of the police searching all around for the murderer and for the money.

'That night was a wild wet night and his mistake was to have stuck the money in a ditch where there was a flood comin' down a drain. It got the money and flooded it out, and some youngsters coming to school in Newtownstewart got £20 notes and £5 notes and £10 notes and they had the fill of their pockets.

'Well, the teacher found the money and asked them where they got it. The next day a young constable come in, wherever he got the information, and he says to the Inspector with a hand on his shoulder, "I arrest you for the murder of William Glass." '

Montgomery was subsequently tried at Omagh. Twice the jury disagreed, but the third time he was found guilty. The day he was hanged was, like the day of the murder itself, 'the wildest day that ever fell from the heavens'.

According to Tom O'Kane another macabre incident concerning Montgomery occurred later.

'He was buried up in the ground of the old gaol. Later they were building a school out at Connorbracken, on the road out to Lammy, and they were using the stones from the old gaol. When they were taking out the stones a horse put its foot into the grave of Montgomery and smashed his jaw bone. There was a stone with the number of his grave, and it is now to be seen in one of the walls of the school at Connorbracken.'

The O'Cahan Arms in Drumquin has one final reminder of that celebrated incident. Along with his collection of old ledgers, a plug

The court-house in Omagh in an earlier era when parking wasn't as problematic as it is today.

of tobacco which is well over 100 years old, and many of the bar fittings which have been handed down through the generations, there is a tall stool which Tom acquired a number of years ago.

'There was an auction in Newtownstewart for a local church and one of the lots was this stool. They told me that it was the stool that William Glass was sitting on in the bank when he was murdered. There wasn't a lot of interest in it and I got it for £15.'

And there it has been from that day to this, in the O'Cahan Arms, except for the time Tom lent it to the Lifford Players when they recreated that story of murder most foul in a recent production.

Iris Brennan

A Shilling and Sixpence in the Toe

On New Year's Eve 1989 I was invited to visit Somme Park at Altnagelvin in Londonderry, an accommodation unit run by the Royal British Legion Housing Association. We had a great party that day, sharing memories of both wartime and peace, with as entertaining a bunch of people as you'd find anywhere.

One of the participants was Iris Brennan, a vivacious, retired lady who loves to live life to the full. Despite the hardship of her early years, and several tragedies in her life, she still finds a lot to laugh about, and is never happier than when sharing that love of life with others.

THE Fountain was called the slums of Londonderry in my day. That's where I was born, in the Protestant slums. And the Catholic slums was the Bogside. The house we lived in was very small. You went into the hall and there was a door at the side of it which led to a big long bedroom where my mother and father slept. We had a big kitchen, no scullery, just an attic upstairs, and the toilet! There was two houses that ran into the one yard. The house next to us had their own toilet, but ours was away round a corner. I used to have to go round in the dark, and I'll tell you it was no joke.

'We had no hot water, just a tank at the back door where we had to wash ourselves in cold water in the morning. My father only worked three days a week, he was just a labourer at a paper mill. I used to love the mornings he came home from work. I had to start early, and he used to call, "Iris, come on, I've got the kettle going." And there was hot water to wash yourself those mornings. It was lovely, you know.'

There wasn't a great deal of privacy for Iris and her family in that small house.

'My mother had a sister who lived with us, and her and I lay in bed together. And my brother lay in the same room as us. There was five years of difference between my brother and I. He lay in one bed,

Iris Brennan

and my aunt and I in the other bed. We had nothin' great, you know, we had just patchwork quilts and we had coats threw over the top. And her and I had this coat, and it had a fur collar on it and she used to say to me, "Right, Iris, turn now", and we'd get the fur collar up round us.

'But on the very, very cold nights, my brother was young, and you know what young blood is, really warm. He'd have been lying in bed and my aunt would have said to me, "It's very cold tonight, come on." And we'd have rolled back his quilt, and she got him by the head and I got him by the feet. And we pushed him into our bed and we got in beside him for the heat. Well in the mornin' he would have wakened with a roar! "Who put me in here?" We used to have some good fun! And my mother had put a table in between the two beds. And as there was no light we just put candles on the table. If you'd seen the three of us kneelin' down, you know, sayin' our prayers. My aunt used to say, "It's like a chapel in the moonlight!"

'In those days we had no electricity. Then we got gas, but not up in the attic. We just had it in the kitchen, as we called it, for we had no living room. There was this big bath, and me mammy used to take this up the stairs, and kettles of water were taken up. But she would have to warn my brother, because in our house we just ran from room to room. Me mammy and daddy never had much privacy. You never knew who would open a door and walk in on you. So she used to say to my brother, "Don't you be goin' up those stairs now, for Iris is havin' a bath."

'And the only place there was any heat was in front of a big open fire, but it wasn't goin' all the time. We couldn't afford it. It was lit in the mornin' when my father came in, and it went out at night.'

If schooldays are the happiest days in the lives of some people, the same would not really have been true for Iris.

'I just went to the one school, Carlisle Road Primary School, the Public Elementary. It's still in existence yet. There was just the four rooms - you had the babies, the senior infants, first class, second class, and then you moved up to the headmaster's. And I always headed the class for slaps for spellin'. That would come as a shock to today's youngsters.

'You had to be in class at ten past nine. If your mother could afford to give you a piece of bread with you, you kept it in your school-bag or attache-cases we used in those days. But you dare not have ate that in class. You got ten minutes break which was to let you out. You couldn't even have got out to the toilet or anything until you had that ten minutes. And by the time you got your chance they were all in it and you never got near it. I used to say, "For God's sake, hurry up!" They had a big bell, and once it rang you had to be in again.

'Then you got out again at half past twelve and you went home. Well, my mother would maybe have had just porridge or soup or something ready for us, because she was out working at the same time. It was a rush home for her too. And then you went back to school and you never got out till the bell again at ten past four.

'But if you didn't do all your lessons, or your homework wasn't good, you were kep' in. You were kep' in until maybe half four or a quarter to five. We had to do it, that was it. And they used the cane, boys and girls. Many's a whack I got of it, no problem at all. And if I'd have gone home and said, "Mammy, I got slapped today", she'd have said,"Well, you didn't get it for nothing. What did ye do?" I'd have said, "Spellings as usual!"

61

Iris Brennan (front row, extreme right) in 1928 taking part in 'The Raggle-Taggle Gypsies Oh' for the school concert at Carlisle Road Public Elementary School.

'I'd be sittin' thinkin', I'll never ever know what I want to be, because unless you were bright nobody bothered about you. You just sailed through, and the only subject in school I ever loved, and we only got it once a month, was geography. We had a board, and maps was hung on the board, and they were swung over to show each country. We used to stand around, and Sammy Wilson handed you his cane and he would have said, "You! Point out such-and-such a place." Well, that I loved. But we only had a half an hour at it once a month. Oh dear, the day I seen that board comin' out, I used to say, "Dear, this is great."

'But many a time I say to myself, "I wonder, if I had got an education like what they're gettin' now, would I have gone on to do somethin' that would have interested me." But most of the days you got sums, spellings, writin'. One thing I will admit, they learned us how to address a letter, put your name and address, you know, "Dear Sir", your commas and all this, if you were writin' a business letter. And readin' too. We were taught our alphabet and tables. You ask any child now of eight or nine, and they couldn't tell you what nine times tables are.

'The first thing you learned was your alphabet, and the first thing you learned to write was your own name. They don't know their alphabet now, I don't believe they do. Mind, knowin' me and my spelling, I was still as dumb as when I started.

'Miss Gault was the teacher of the babies. Miss Hamilton took senior infants. Miss Ebbie Weir, she took the next one, and Mr Sammy Wilson was the headmaster. He was a right bugger, especially if he'd a drink in him. He just sat up at that desk and he leaned into you, and by God he made you work. Having said all that, I wasn't that interested in school, but I never missed a day. Anything I've learned, I've learned since I've come away from school. I can read. I read books now, which I never done before. But then I never had time to do it before. There was nothing really in school.

'They weren't the happiest days of my life … maybe in some ways they were. And there was nothing really to come home to, you know, that I'd 've said, "Oh God, I'm glad I'm goin' home, Mammy'll have a lovely dinner for me", or something like that. There was none of that because we hadn't the money to have a dinner. We had a good dinner on Sunday, that was about the only day we had any kind of a good dinner.

'It was just a sheer existence. I only had the one rig of clothes, a good coat and frock and shoes and hat when I went to church on a Sunday. And I'll tell you another thing about a Sunday. I got up on Sunday morning, my brother and I, and we were sent out to Sunday school. Now that was down in the Strand, we had a mile to walk to it. When we came out of Sunday school my father was standing waiting for us and we went into church. We came home from there and we got our dinner and I went down then to the Salvation Army, and I stayed there from two to three. That was another Sunday school. We came out of there and we went up to the Baptists in Carlisle Road from three to four. We came home then and we got our tea, and then I went to the Church of Ireland service from seven to eight.

'From there I went down to the 'Dippers' at the foot of the

Fountain. Those were the people that dipped you. You were christened, fully submerged. Then it was home at last and me Mammy used to say, "You'll only have to go to bed. If there was only any place else I could send ye."'

But all this 'good living' paid some dividends to Iris and her friends.

'Of course, we went so we could go on the excursions. You could collect the free tickets they gave out so they'd take us on the excursions. We got to Portrush and Buncrana, usually on a Saturday. The organisations carried their urns and all, and the tea was made on the beach, and you got a bag of buns. That was your day out, singing hymns on the beach.'

In the days when a lot of families never had the chance to take a holiday those trips were a popular substitute.

Just as in Derry, water carts operated on the streets of Belfast and provided impromptu entertainment for the children who couldn't afford trips to the seaside.

'That's the way it was for a lot of people then. There wasn't much in the way of holidays. Me father never was fond of travelling anywhere. He was a kind of a home bird, but a lovable person, full

of fun. I've never heard my father or mother, or sister or brother, curse. I was the only one that cursed, but I didn't do it at home or I'd have been clipped. Mammy was more or less house-proud. She was all for buildin' her home, which wasn't a bad thing. It ended up we had a beautiful wee home. I had to do exactly the same as what my mother had to do. My first child was born when I was only seventeen. It was born with the bare boards on the floor. They had to roll it up in a bit of flannel just to keep it warm till I got clothes for it.'

That was in the depression years of the early thirties, when many women were forced to seek whatever work was available, because jobs for men were even harder to find.

'When I left school at fourteen, I got a job in Kennedy's, sweepin' the floors. It was a small shirt factory down in Magazine Street. Shirt makin' was the main industry in those days. That's why some people called it the Maiden City. All the women worked out. When the factories opened their doors to let the people out it was just a seethin' mass of women. Very few men worked in the cuttin' rooms. If you married a shirt cutter you got one of the best tradesmen in Derry. You were elected. That's what they said, and I should know for I married one. To get a job, well, my mother had to take me round

Belonging to a Sunday school before the war was a guaranteed way of getting to the seaside. Organised outings, to Donegal, Portstewart or Portrush, were some compensation for the lack of holidays for many children.

the day before I was fourteen to all the factories to see if they could start me. So Kennedy's was the only one that would take me in, just sweepin' floors now, with a brush. No shovel or nothin', or anything like that. You know what you call a potato sack; well, I had to lift the dust into that and pull it out into the yard. Me first pay in that factory was two-and-six a week, workin' from half past eight till six at night.

'I had to hand that all in. Me mother knew what my wage was, so I had to give her the half-crown an' I didn't get anything back. In them days you just played around the streets, skipping or swinging on lamp-posts. They used to have shutters up on the windows, and you'd have gone from one end of the street to the other jumpin' up on them and swingin' on the shutters, you know, and we'd have gone up round the Walls at night and played up there. We'd have played with stones, not firin' stones like, just playin' buildin' wee houses. Maybe you'd have got the brush on a nice summer night, and you'd have said, "Come on, we'll play wee houses," ye know, and you'd have swep' up and built your house.'

Like many of her contemporaries, Iris learnt to become an adult early in life. And most days were the same, with very little difference even at more festive times.

'Christmas and birthdays were not like today. They were nothin' special. At Christmas you got a toy, and you always hung your stockin' up on the mantlepiece. And I always remember you got a shilling and sixpence in the toe, and an apple and an orange, and then maybe a wee bag of sweets at the top. That was your stockin'. One year ye'd have got a doll, and the next year a pram. I had a doll, I think it was a new one me mother bought me. I was always very careful. I had it for years and years. I never had a name for it. It was a black doll and I idolised it. No one ever had a black doll and I'll never know where me mother got it. When we got on a bit she had a glass case in the living room, and that's where I kept that doll.

'I remember she gave it away one time to someone, and I broke my heart over it. I never got it back. Some child took a fancy to it and me mother gave it to her. And birthdays, they just passed. Ye'd say, "I'm thirteen today", and that was it.

'Well, I left Kennedy's, but when I moved up from Sunday school to the Bible class the teacher owned a factory, and my aunt worked in it. So me mother took me down to see him and he said he would take me in. And my aunt that worked in it was a front stitcher, workin' on the fronts of shirts. That was a skilled job, and he says, "Well, I'll take Iris in, but I can't pay anyone to learn her the trade that she wants to go to." So my mother had to pay my aunt to teach

Regatta day on the Foyle.
Well dressed locals cool off.

me my trade. She gave her 2s.6d. or 3s. a week to learn me my trade. I only got a fortnight to learn it because that was all my mother could afford, then I had to go on earnin' me own wage.

'So I became a front stitcher. Everybody in the factory had a skill. There was what was called the fitters; they fitted the shirt. There was the hemmers, there was the side seamers, there was the banders, the collar workers, and the cuffers. That made up the whole shirt.

'I'm talking about them days, not like today. They were all hand made. They came up from the cuttin' room in a roll. The hemmer got it first. She opened it up; she hemmed the front and the back. There was vents went into the front. That was her job. That then came to me, that bundle of work, and I took out the fronts only, the part I was workin' at, and the straps. And I laid in me straps. Then I folded that up, and when I'd done a dozen I took them up to the girl in charge. It took me an hour to do a dozen, and I got sixpence ha'penny for a dozen of work.

Girls like Iris worked in cramped conditions at their sewing benches in the shirt factories of the Maiden City.

'My wage at the end of the week would have been about twelve shillings. That was the most I could earn. And bein' only fourteen that was hard work. Every week I handed that to me mother, maybe some weeks I'd have got an extra one-an'-six, and I'd 'ave kept that and never let on. Me mother bought all my clothes, stockin's and the like. You just had to wear what your mother bought for you. Whether you liked it or it suited you or not, that was it. She bought things wherever she could get them cheapest, and she kept us right and tidy.

'I walked two miles from home to where I worked, an' I had to be in at half past eight in the mornin' dead on. You were locked out if you were late. There were no tea breaks or nothing. Very few girls smoked in those days; they couldn't afford them. It wasn't the done thing. You walked it up home at half past twelve for lunch, and you had to be back again for two o'clock. You worked then from two till six with just ten minutes of a break in between. Again there was no tea nor nothing. If you had a piece with you, you went into the toilets and ate it.

'There was no such things as dining-rooms, everything was taken into the toilets. Maybe the odd night you'd have to work in. That meant you'd have to walk home for your tea to be back again by seven and work till nine. And you worked on a Saturday morning from half past eight till half twelve. Nobody would do it now, not a girl would do it now.'

And the working conditions Iris describes would hardly be acceptable these days either.

'You'd nothin' but a round stool, no back or nothin' on it, you just sat on that stool. There was a bench, just wider than me. That was what I had to work at. I had a box at the side that stood on four feet, where I kep' me work, and that was me bench and that was me machine. We had to work to a certain stitch, a fifteen stitch it was called. It was a very small stitch. You had a thing up on a wheel that you could have adjusted to a bigger stitch. Well, if you adjusted to a bigger stitch, you know, to make the thing go a bit faster, you had that all to rip out again.

'The bench went down into a bevel. You dropped your work into that, and pulled it out and finished it off, and folded it and rolled it up and put it into your box. The floor was littered with rags, because you see we always had to pare our work. When I worked in Lloyd, Attree and Smyth's we had power to run the machinery, but the lightin' was gas, and nobody was allowed to touch them because of the mantles. You would have broke the mantles, so we had to wait till one of the boys from the cuttin' room would come down and light the gas for us.

'Sometimes you would have had good material but sometimes it was bad, limey material, and when you were machinin' - with the rate it was goin' - the lime was comin' up roun' you. Your hair would have been white with lime, and you were breathin' this all in. Well, then the girl would come round - we called her charwoman - and she would have swep' all that, and all that dust was goin' up round you. You just got up off your stool and stepped back and let her sweep out your place.

Mr McKinney, one of the managers at the Rosemount factory, with one of his supervisors and the men who were 'the best tradesmen in Derry'.

'We'd no overalls either, you wore your own clothes and they got covered in it too. We used to wear a wee pad - you made it yourself. It tied round your hand because the heat of the wheel would have burnt you. You were workin' with your head down all the time and sometimes you'd have got the needle through your finger. Maybe, if you lifted your eye when you were up close to the foot of the machine, the needle would come down. I remember the needle comin' down through my finger. It always broke because you'd automatically pull your hand back.

'They'd just take you out on the fire-escape and set you up on a stool. Then they'd send for the mechanic and he'd come down with a pair of pliers. He just got it and pulled the needle out and you went back to work again. No doctors, no nurses. And sometimes he'd a job findin' the end of it.

'I ended up as a supervisor of a factory, and I knew what it was like. I went through it. When I was supervisor I had the best girls, and I run that factory like clockwork. I could go from one end of it to the other and see the whole order out and no problems at all. I can make a shirt right through from beginning to end. Now my machine, that I learned my trade on, was just an ordinary sewing machine. The hemmers had the same machine as mine but they had a guide for folding the work in to get the hem to come round. Then there was what they call the post-fellin' machines. Now they were big machines that came forward to you. They had two guides on them and they were for side-seamers, joining the backs and the fronts of the shirts together. The cuffers had a guide too because they had to do the stitchin' round the cuff. The banders and the collar workers, they had guides too for to go round the edge of your collar.

'I must have been about 27 or 28 when I became a supervisor, so it took me 14 years working to get there.'

The money she brought in was important to Iris because she had become a bride while still in her teens, and indeed bore her first child when she was only 17.

'When we got married we had no place to go. In those days you went out and looked for some place to live. We got a room, that's what you called it, just a room. It was just a bedroom and I had the use of a kitchen.

'But I was never a very good cook. I remember the first soup I made him I nearly poisoned him with salt. And God love him, he ate it! He was a shirt cutter and that was a good job. So we took on a house at fifteen bob a week, a wee new house, because my first baby was due. We didn't have much, only a bed and a wardrobe and a chair in the bedroom, and a table and four chairs downstairs. I didn't even have a cooker, just the top of one.

'Well, the baby was born at home and I'd very little for it. My mother was never the motherly type. She would never have said, "I'll buy something for the baby." When it was a month old I had to take it to Belfast, to hospital. It would take me all day to tell you what I went through. I didn't know a sinner, and I walked from one end of Belfast to the other and not a bite in my stomach. I hadn't a ha'penny or a penny for the tram, and I sat in that hospital all day. I remember the day the baby went through its operation I was sittin' downstairs, and I'd nothin' but a wee raincoat on me, and in those days you wore berets.

'I was sittin' on a wooden seat and I was there from eight o'clock in the morning. About two o'clock the Sister came down, and she shouts, "Mrs Smith?" And I stood up. "Mrs Smith. My God," she says, "you're just a child. Are you the mother of William Smith? Well, you can go up and see him, he's just out of theatre."

'I went up and I stayed with him. He was only four weeks old. Well, I done that for a week and, honest to God, I don't believe that full week I had three cups of tea in me. I never knew what it was to have a meal, I couldn't afford it. I was stayin' with my father's cousins and he was a bachelor and he had two nephews livin' with him. I didn't know them from Adam, and I was scared stayin' in a house with three men. So that was what kept me out during the day. And I went to bed at night when I came home.

'But it was pathetic that any young girl should have to go through that. I stayed a fortnight and my husband couldn't afford to come up and see me. But we brought the baby back and we went to his mother's house. She says to me, "You know, Iris, I don't think the baby's well at all." That was on the 12 August, and on the 14th he was dead.

'When the baby was buried I went back to work again, and do you know, within a week I was pregnant again. By the time my second baby was born I had that wee house of ours furnished. No carpets, you know, just oil cloth. I worked that hard and I mind me daddy sittin' down that proud because my wee house was shinin'.

'So I had another wee boy, and I stayed a year out of work with him, and then my husband's aunt was gettin' put out of her room. She was stone-deaf and his mother wanted me to get a bigger house and to take her in — which I did. I moved then to a house with three bedrooms, and I brought this old lady with me. She was out working as a washerwoman in a shirt factory. And I says to her, would it not be better if she looked after the baby for me, and I went out, for I could earn more money than her.

'She agreed to that and I went out. But then I got pregnant again. I'm tellin' you, it was a good job the war broke out! I used to tell me mother if it wasn't for the war I'd have had a tribe of weans. But I still worked on. This baby was six months old whenever war was declared. My man was in the Territorials and I says, "Does that mean you'll be called away?" Now, he had two pounds seventeen a week, and with what I was bringin' in, we were doin' nicely. September the war broke out, October or November they were called up.

'Most of them were married men, just a few singles, an' I suppose they thought, "We'll get away from the wives for a couple of weeks over in England." They wakened up a few days later when they realised they were bound for Egypt. And they were there for five years. So I never seen him for five years. But it meant that the two pounds seventeen fell to one pound ten. That's what the government allowed me to keep myself and two children. Thirty bob a week. But I went out to work right enough, no family allowance then or nothin'.

'Well, the war was a different kettle of fish. I was only 22. I didn't neglect the children, don't get me wrong, but I do and I always did love dancin'. I used to go to the dances, to the Corinthian Hall, the Memorial Hall, the Tower Ballroom, the Clarendon, the Britannia Hall. There were more dance halls than enough. And the bands. There were the McIntyres, Joe and Gay. Then the Yanks came in, but the British Navy were the best dancers of the lot.

'The Yanks, when they came with the Jitterbug and all, they thought they were the bees' knees, but I never liked the Yanks. Mind, I could still do the Jitterbug if I was put to it, even at my age.

'After five years my husband came back. He was always a very jealous type of man from whenever I started goin' with him when I was 14. He wouldn't even let me sit beside another man in the picture house. To be quite honest with you, I had quite a tough time with him. He was a big six-footer and he gave me a bit of abuse. There was nowhere to run in them days, you had to stick it out. I remember his father saying to me, "Iris, if you don't take your feet now you never will. Take your stand."'

Iris did take a stand and despite some of the difficulties, things did seem to improve for a while. Her husband left the shirt factory and got another job at British Oxygen. But she became aware that he was falling into deep depression.

'He started to clam up. He kept everything to himself, and though we had always talked to each other I found that he was all closed in. One night we had a bit of an argument and the next morning I

Lloyd, Attree and Smyth's centenary dinner in 1957.

was getting ready to go out to work at nine o'clock. He'd already been out and had come back home. I asked him what he was doing and he told me he'd come back for his glasses.

'So I asked him to give me a lift down to my work, and when we got there he said, "Are you not going to say goodbye to me?" I looked at him for a minute and said, "What'll I say goodbye for?" And I closed the car door and went in to work. During the day I kept thinkin' that I'd been a bit nasty to him that morning, so I decided to buy him a couple of shirts and take them home to him.

'He always used to wait for me outside, but when I got out he wasn't there. I started walkin' and lookin' back, and as I did my temper started rising. But when I got home, I found him there - dead. I ran out squealin' into the street. It tore me to shreds and there was a very big funeral for him for he was very well known. I had a lot of help from people but it didn't bring him back to me.'

That was in 1965 and it took time for Iris to get over the experience. Later, though, she found another husband, and an idyllic relationship.

'I never went out for six months, and then I went out for a message and was introduced to the man who became my second husband. He wanted to see me home and I wouldn't let him. Three weeks later he told me that he was going to marry me, and I told him he was not! He was a Chief Petty Officer in the Navy, and not long after I met him he was posted to Singapore. "Will you marry me and go out there with me?"

'But I was dilatory and still said no. The day he was to leave I came out of work and he was standin' there.

'"Are you not going to Singapore," I said.

'"I am indeed, but not before we get engaged."

'Well, he took me down to Fallers and bought me an engagement ring. Just after he went away, I was invited to a christening on board his ship by the captain. Before I went ashore the captain asked me why I hadn't gone out to Singapore with Jimmy. I told him that I wasn't sure of him and didn't know if he was already married. And I'll always remember his reply.

'"No, he's not married. He's one of the best chaps on board this ship. I can vouch for him."

'I knew that if I meant as much as he said I did, he'd be back for me. He was away for almost a year and a half, and when he came back I was able to meet his family in Yorkshire at his sister's wedding. One of my sons was about to get married at that time too, and Jimmy stood in for his father. That was on the 19 August, and Jimmy brought out his diary. I didn't know what he was doing until he told me, "We're getting married on the 7 October." Well, he was the best man on God's earth, the best fella that ever walked on two feet. He came out of the Navy after 25 years and was working down in Dupont's as an engineer. He loved it, but one morning when he got up out of bed he was standin' there and I looked at him and said, "It's not just your day, love." And he looked a wee bit drawn, you know, and I says, "Are you not just feelin' up to the mark?"

'"No I don't think so, Iris," he says.

'Well, he had his breakfast, and I kissed him goodbye and told him to watch himself and God bless. I waved to him till he was round the corner. Some of his working clothes were on the bed so I decided to wash them as it was a nice day. I was just washing the clothes when I heard the knock at the door.

'I went out and I could see figures at the vestibule door. It was the man next door and his wife. Now, he worked in Dupont's, but for the life of me I couldn't tell who were the two men standing behind him. I said, "Och, hullo Mervyn." And he just came forward and he got me by the shoulders. There was a big long hall I had, and he moved me down it. On the way down I said to him, "It's Jimmy. There's something wrong with Jimmy." But they waited till they got me into the lounge, and when I was sitting down the man from the back says, "Mrs Brennan, I'm very sorry to have to tell you, but your husband's dead." Well I just don't know. I says it couldn't be, let me see him. But they told me they couldn't and that everything possible had been done for him. He just went down like that without one word of warning, and yet he was only 44 years of age. And that was the end of my Jimmy.'

Iris had to start rebuilding her life again. But her strength of character stood her in good stead and she learnt to start living all over again. Now, in her seventies, and looking very much younger than her years, she lives in a very happy and active retirement. And whenever there's something to celebrate, or there's a gathering in the offing, she'll be there, the life and soul of the party.

Harry Currie

Sore Heads and Donkey's Lugs

> Harry Currie is very much a survivor. A lively and active man in his nineties he runs three pensioners' clubs, and has little time for those who say they feel old when they reach normal retirement age. His experience of life ranges from his character-building days in Ireland's oldest surviving Boys' Brigade Company, 9th Belfast, in the days immediately before the First World War; his service in that war; the struggle to make a living in the twenties; and the happier days when he worked on the trams and trolley-buses which were once a familiar sight on the streets of the city.

'I WAS born at number 9 Walnut Place, just off Donegall Pass, on 31 December 1897. My parents had five children, but two died in infancy. I was the youngest, and am the only survivor.

'The first school I went to was the old National school at the bottom of the Ormeau Road. They only knocked it down recently. It was a mixed school with three classrooms and the headmaster was a Mr Carter. I mustn't have been all that happy there for my mammy moved me round from time to time, to McClure Street and All Saints for a while. I ended up in the McQuiston School at Donegall Pass and left school for good when I was fourteen.

'I don't suppose I was a bad youngster, nor were those I grew up with, though we were often chased by the peelers. They didn't like some of the things we got up to in the streets, like tying ropes to the old gas lamp-posts and swinging round them. Today's youngsters would be amazed at what kept us happy then.

'There was 'Churchy and One Over', where you leant on a window sill or against a wall and your mates jumped on your back to see how many you could carry. There was 'Piggy, which you played with a couple of pieces of stick. One was used to strike the other, and many's a window got broke that way. 'Kick the tin' made a change from playing with a hanky ball. You chose one of the gang to kick a tin as far as he could while the others hid. They had to try to get out

Harry Currie.

of hiding and kick the tin away again before you could spot them. If you saw them coming you called out their names.

'And we got to know which of the parlour houses had courtin' couples in them. If they'd left the sash window up a wee bit, we would sneak up and let the blind up with a rush! They got a shock and we got another chase!'

Some of the streets produced their own makeshift football teams and Harry played for Botanic along with his friend Billy McCleery from nearby Rutland Street. Billy went on to greater things in the

Camping with the Boys' Brigade at Ganaway involved a certain amount of physical activity. By the 1920s Lieutenant Currie was taking on more responsibility in the movement.

world of sport, from Linfield to Blackburn Rovers and eventually he became an Irish international. Harry sums it up with a laugh, 'He had a head for it. I didn't!'

But much of Harry's time as a young man was taken up with the Boys' Brigade, and he has happy memories of the company camps at Castlerock or Millisle, or at Ganaway or Ballyferris for the big Battalion camps.

'I joined the 9th Belfast company in 1908 and you paid 7s. 6d. for a week's camp, and that included your train fare.

'At camp the day started early with reveille at 6.30 a.m. The band would march round the tents to wake all the boys up. Those that didn't got a rattle round the legs with the cane from the Battalion chaplain, the Rev. R. H. S. Cooper, to help them on their way. And when some of us went to wash in cold water out of a large barrel we found that we had blackened faces.

'It was a practical joke that was often played, to blacken someone's face with Cherry Blossom boot polish while they slept. And it was hard to wash it off in cold water. When washing was over you had to fold your blankets to the pattern laid down for you, ready for the daily inspection of the tents which took place immediately after breakfast and morning prayers. If you'd done it badly you were put on fatigues and you might be sent to the cookhouse to peel spuds and take the eyes out of them. When you were on fatigues you wore a yellow armband to identify you. At the end of the week there was a prize awarded for the best kept tent at the camp.

'After the daily inspection you were dismissed and the day was your own. It was usually filled with sport, tug o' war, bathing or football. The tents were laid out in 'streets' called A street, B street and so on. There was even a D street! A football league was organised between the different streets.

'The day ended at ten o'clock when the gates were closed. If you'd been out and got back late names were taken. The buglers sounded retreat, cocoa was served with 'the grogger', a big slab of biscuit, and 'lights out' came as soon as evening prayers were over.'

In those days many young men followed the trade or profession of their fathers, but not Harry.

'My father had been a watchmaker and jeweller at Sharman D. Neill's in Donegall Place. I still remember the place where he worked. There was even a clock in the handle of the door. He died young, at the age of 52, and I could never have done the work he did. All that close work was very hard on the eyes, and the benzine they used to clean the watches and clocks was bad for the chest and the eyes.'

Harry wasn't prepared to follow in his father's footsteps and on leaving school became a message boy for Wright and Hunter's in Arthur Street.

'In them days there were a lot of class shops with important and wealthy customers. A lot of business people would have got their work done there. On the first floor were the cabinetmakers, above them the French polishers, on the third floor the upholsterers, and in a separate room the upholsteresses. And they all had to work hard. It was 8.00 a.m. to 6.30 p.m. Monday to Friday, and till one o'clock on Saturdays. You got the twelfth week off and two days at Christmas and Easter.

'I was paid five shillings a week to deliver stuff round the town, or collect hinges, screw nails or locks for wardrobes. And I can still smell the glue they used. The glue pot was kept on a gas burner in a tank of water. You had to keep an eye on it for the cabinetmakers would have been after you if you let it boil over.'

Presiding over the entire workforce was Mr Wright himself, with a reputation as something of a crosspatch. He was very sharp.

'The old lift was hard to work right; it was hard to judge stopping it. Many's a bang was heard when you got it wrong at the top or bottom of the shaft. Then the foreman came out and the culprit got the sharp end of his tongue.

'We set our time by the hooter at Ross's mineral water factory behind us, though you'd have heard it all over town. It blew like a train. And every night at six our own Miss Ross used to send for me to post the mail in Arthur Square.'

Others Harry can remember are people like 'Dummy' Johnston.

'He must have been related to the hooter - you could have heard him at the other end of the street.' And Gubby Ward: 'He had too much to say. He knew all about the trade inside out, and at the end knew nothing.'

But it was with Wright and Hunter that Harry, at the age of sixteen, became an apprentice.

'I got a chance of my trade there and they took me on as an apprentice upholsterer. Six years it took in them days, though later you only did five. And when you'd served your time they paid you off, unless they had work for you.

'They really made furniture then. Everything stitched into position, canvas, hessian and calico, and hair and fibre filling. Pullin' it this way and pullin' it that, it was hard on the fingers but you never noticed. You had to be exact. And they were built to last. There were nine springs to a chair. Not like today with only four or five. Even the chair backs were sprung. Nowadays they are only padded. A good suite of furniture then, covered in moquette or tapestry or French velour with silk cording would have sold for £20 or £25.'

Pointing at one of his present day chairs Harry adds, 'That old thing there cost me £200 and its not comfortable at all. Besides, modern chairs are too low. Nine inch legs were far better.'

'The frames were made at Luney's in Dawson Street, who would show their stock sizes. Customers could chose from these or from their catalogue. And if it wasn't in stock they'd have had it made up.'

But before his apprenticeship ended many of Harry's friends had gone off to war, and he decided to follow them.

'It was 1916 and on every street corner there were large posters of Kitchener pointing at you. "Your King and Country need YOU!" they said, so I went to the old Town Hall in Victoria Street and volunteered for the army. I was given a rifle, a uniform, food and accommodation, and sixpence a day. I left Belfast on the Liverpool Boat with a big, hard sergeant to greet me. I was half out to sea when I wished I was back home again. All the young fellas were joining up all over. The boat was packed and there was nowhere to lie down.

'I was sent to the Mechanical Transport Royal Army Corps and, after basic training at Norwood and Sydenham in London, was posted to Bulford Camp to join a unit to go overseas. We left for France in December 1917 on board RMS *Aragon*, a mail boat converted to carry troops. When we arrived off Le Havre we weren't allowed to disembark, and just sat there for two or three days. Nobody knew what was going on because all troop movements were secret.

'But one of the sergeants was in the know. He came round and within minutes the whole ship knew we were for Egypt. There were thousands on board and the first thing I had to learn was how to cope with a hammock. It was shockin'. I nearly always fell out gettin' in, but I suppose it was better than sleeping on the deck. We reached St Paul's Bay, Malta, to take on supplies, and escorted by five destroyers - two Japanese and three British - set sail to become part of the big push on the Holy Land under General Allenby. That was the big idea, but we were never to be part of it because 30 miles off the coast at Alexandria we were torpedoed.

An historic photograph taken by one of Harry Currie's fellow survivors in the dramatic moments after the RMS Aragon was torpedoed off Alexandria in Egypt in December 1917.

'I was down below, two decks below, playing draughts with another soldier. We heard a thud and felt a big jolt. We had no idea what it was so we went up on deck to see. The news that we had been torpedoed by a submarine spread quickly. There was no panic as we took up our stations, putting on our life-jackets and taking our shoes off. There were ropes hanging down the ship's sides leading to lifeboats and rafts in the water.

'Only some of the boats could be launched because of the angle of the Aragon. Not everyone got off, and I still have a vivid memory of a terrible situation that I witnessed. Some soldiers had been caught breaking regulations earlier, like smoking against orders, and had been locked up in the brig which was a sort of locked area up on the top deck. There was a guard on duty and I said to him, "Aren't you going to shoot the lock off and let them out?" But he said, "I daren't do that. I have no orders. I'm on guard here - I'll have to wait till I'm told."

'As far as I know those men went down with the ship, which sank within fifteen minutes of being hit. The last thing I remember before going over the side was hearing the Captain crying out, "Every man for himself, and God be with you." I heard later that he too had gone down with the ship.'

Harry was pulled down by the undertow, and despite being unable to swim cannot remember any feeling of panic. He had been taking part in confirmation classes on board, and he said a prayer as he went under. The next thing he remembers is being pulled up into a lifeboat which was so overcrowded that it too was in danger of sinking. One of the escorting destroyers, HMS *Attack*, took them all on board and many of the rescued soldiers took off their lifejackets and threw them away. The cords on Harry's had knotted and he couldn't get his off.

This saved his life because disaster struck again. Ten minutes after being rescued HMS *Attack* was herself torpedoed, and almost immediately broke in two. One part of the ship sank straight away, but he was on the other half.

'I was on the part that floated, and there was a lot of fighting for lifebelts. Then I was in the sea again and, supported by the life-jacket that I was still wearing, I floated for a while until I lost consciousness. I came to on board a minesweeper and was talking to someone lying on the deck beside me when someone else said, "You needn't be talking to him - he's gone."

'It was December and when we were landed in Alexandria I was very cold. There were rows of blankets on the shore and when I went to pick one up an MP told me not to touch them, saying, "Them's all dead bodies." A lot of people died in that double sinking.'

This incident meant that Harry and his unit missed General Allenby's assault on the Holy Land. He did serve in south-east Europe, and in the Middle East, and though the war ended in 1918 didn't return home again until April 1920. On board a captured German ship, the *Brandenburg*, he sailed through the Suez canal and all the way to India. Eventually he was de-mobbed in England and

it was back again to complete his apprenticeship with Wright and Hunter's.

The junction of Royal Avenue and North Street.

But unemployment was widespread in the early 20's and like many others he was paid off. Willing to try anything he became a breadserver for the Bloomfield Bakery.

'They gave me a horse-drawn van, a two-wheeler, and sent me off to do the rounds of the lower Ormeau Road. So I spent some time becoming an expert in Melodion loaves, Turnovers, Sore Heads, Donkey's Lugs, Paris buns and the lot. I learnt how the 'Baker's Dozen' got its name - 13 pastries for a shilling. And you used a long rake to take as much off the cart and put it on the tray so that when you went to the door they'd always buy more than they meant to.

'To get that job I had to find £50 as a deposit to cover losses and bad debts. If the amount owing to the breadman came near to the limit the checkers would warn you to get it in. I was lucky to get the £50 to get started. The Rev. H. G. Maturin, Minister of All Saints, gave me a recommendation, and arranged a bank loan. I paid it back monthly, and if I'd any extra coming in, I paid more back.'

But Harry was operating in an area where he was well known, and the competition was fierce. McWatters, Barney Hughes, McCombe's, Mercers, Parks as well as Inglis and Ormeau were all after the same custom, and he found some resentment that he was trying to take business away from some of the others. So after a year he packed it in.

He decided to become a self-employed upholsterer, and took over a room attached to the stables in Eblana Street, off Cromwell Road. With handbills printed he set off to look for clients. But by now cut-price shops were arriving in Belfast.

'Cavendish did me a lot of harm when they set up in Donegall Place. They had a big advertisement which offered to furnish your house for five shillings a week. And they were selling three-piece suites for between £10 and £12. When I went round to give an estimate of maybe £3 to cover a seat, which I needed because of the cost of the springs and hessian and so on, nobody was interested. So within a year I gave up.'

It was one of Harry's customers who suggested a different career.

The most famous city junction was Castle Junction, a busy place where most city tram routes converged.

'Why not try the trams? You'd have no trouble there, being an ex-serviceman.' There were 40 applicants for the job of conductor, and after passing a test where he had to add up columns of tuppences and pennies, Harry was accepted. Sandy Row was one of the city's

For those able to afford a little luxury, the pre-war Carlton provided a suitably sophisticated setting. The Carlton was one of a number of well appointed restaurants which flourished in Belfast between the wars.

biggest depots and here he started his new career doing holiday duties.

'You worked with a different driver every two weeks and were sent on routes all over the city. The dawn shift was the tough one when you reported in at 4.30 a.m. to check the duty board which gave you your runs and times. They checked you out leaving the depot, and you had to be on time going through Castle Junction where most of the cross-town lines passed. The dawn shift ended at 11.30 a.m. and many's a morning you were half sleepin' before you went to bed. But you worked hard on the early shift. There were always plenty of passengers - timekeepers for the shipyard and the factories, policemen, nurses, milkmen and even tramway staff themselves.'

Many of the old red trams had uncomfortable slatted wooden seats but for many years few people would have thought of complaining. Later, though, after letters to the *Belfast Telegraph* some trams were modernised and softer seats were provided. If the main reason for having a conductor on board was to collect the fares, there were many other responsibilities which conductors had to take on. Destination boards were carried on the sides of the trams and they indicated which routes the trams were following. Even so, when he was stopped outside the City Hall, Harry got used to being asked, 'Are ye goin' up Bedford Street?' even though it was written in large letters on the side of the tram!

And when the tram reached its destination it was the conductor's job to swing the trolley round for the return journey. Less of a problem during the day, it was a hazardous business in the dark.

'You had to keep an eye out for the motorists, for many's a conductor was knocked down at night.'

There was one place in the city where some passengers had to change from 'red' to 'green'. At Chichester Park on the Antrim Road a private company with its own electric power supply took over from the city trams, and its green trams served the top part of the Antrim Road.

Being a conductor for something like 29 years, Harry got to know many of the personalities of the company, especially the inspectors.

Donegall Place on Rag Day 1935. An occasion when even the trams had difficulty making their way through the centre of town.

One of them, Inspector Cherry, was a formidable character, though Harry got on well with him.

'Very few of the drivers or conductors liked him, though I always found him strict but honest, and he would always give you good advice. "Watch that driver. He's very crooked and'll get you into bother leavin' before your time." People don't realise that it was the conductor who was in charge of the tram, not the driver. Cherry was

always reminding us of it. Then there was Inspector Henderson, known as 'Half-a-minute' Henderson because he had time on the brain. He was a fidgety man, and as he waited for your tram to arrive you could always see him taking his watch in and out of his pocket over and over again. But then most of the inspectors were very hot on time.

'Joe Black was known as 'Two watch'. The trouble was his two watches never showed the same time, but it didn't stop him finding fault, and his favourite saying was, "You're half a minute sharp." They also made sure that all your passengers had tickets, and some would be quick to report you if they found any without.'

It wasn't always easy for Harry and his colleagues to take the money off all the passengers. On the shipyard runs the trams carried a lot more people than they were designed for. Every available space would be jam packed, with men hanging on anywhere they could get a hold.

'I got them all, or at least as many as I could, but you'd often see

Gone but not forgotten. A once familiar sight in the old Smithfield Market.

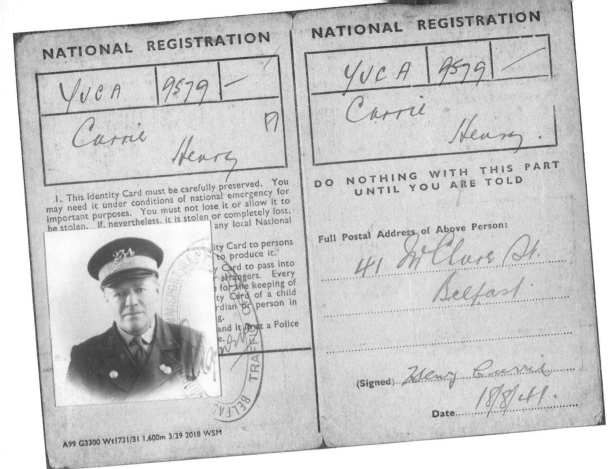

Identity cards were once part of life. This one includes the only existing picture of Harry Currie in his tram conductor's uniform.

men jumping off when I got near. I suppose they did the same on the next tram to come along.

'But I made the job a picnic for myself. Some conductors argued with the public and got themselves into difficulties. I never did. The usual complaint was early in the morning when passengers offered half a crown or a ten bob note for a tuppenny fare and you could quickly run out of change.'

When the Second World War started in September 1939 there was a great deal of complacency in Belfast. Nobody foresaw any real risk of air raids so far away from the main action, but on Easter Tuesday 1941 the first big raid hit Belfast and widespread damage was caused, mainly in the north of the city. The Antrim Road and Crumlin Road depots were both hit. Harry remembers those days, and nights, very well.

'I was told to come in early to help keep the trams running. I got to Sandy Row depot at five in the morning. Sam Carlisle was the manager then, and he and his inspectors had already been out surveying the damage. Lack of power was the main problem. There were wires down and damage to the lines in a number of places. But repairs were made as quickly as possible and in many parts of the

90

city the trams kept to a near-normal schedule.'

Even without the air raids, wartime operations gave tram crews additional difficulties and they were issued with identity cards because of the curfew which had been imposed.

'Because of the blackout there were covers on the lamps inside the trams and they gave out only a glimmer of light. You can imagine what it was like trying to collect the fares and give out the right change in those conditions. And calling out the names of the stops in the dark was very difficult. I can still remember some of the places I had to identify. On the Ormeau Road it was, "Next stop Ormeau Avenue... Donegall Pass... McClure Street... Agincourt Avenue... Ormeau Park... South Parade..." and then, "the Ulster Cricket Grounds."'

Not every conductor bothered to call out the street names as Harry did, and it didn't go unnoticed. He was commended for it by the then Traffic Manager, Mr Craig.

Upper Ann Street in 1948, leading directly on to Queen's Bridge. Trams occupied most of the roadway, possible in the days when few people owned their own private cars.

The first trolleybuses appeared on the streets of Belfast in the late thirties. This one, in splendid isolation, was pictured on the Albertbridge Road in 1942. The absence of other traffic was presumably due in part to petrol rationing. A decade later buses gradually ousted the trams from the streets of the city.

'At certain times special, decorated trams ran through Belfast. If there was a Coronation, or on Empire Day, and when the war ended both VE Day and VJ Day had decorated trams on the streets to celebrate the end of the war.

'One other wartime memory I have is of some of the weddings that took place. There was a lot of jollification on the streets and when it got a bit out of order the military would arrive. People just flew in whatever door was open. They flew up the hall and hid, then they'd juke out when the coast was clear.

'But it wasn't long after the war that the trams began to disappear from the streets of Belfast. In 1953 more buses took over, and the last trams ran on 28 February 1954 when twelve of them travelled in procession from the Queen's Road up to the Ardoyne depot. At first I was transferred to work as conductor on the diesel buses. It made a big difference the way the driver was able to move in and out of the traffic. But I had to speed up to get the fares collected, as it was a lot faster than on the trams I was used to.

'Then more trolley buses were brought in, and I was transferred again. They had the electric speed and were very quick off the mark. For conductors they were worse still. I had to double up to keep on top of things.'

In 1962, when he reached the age of 65, Harry had to retire from Belfast Corporation. There were no concessions for former tramway men, though he quickly found that bus conductors wouldn't take his fare, and even the inspectors turned a blind eye to his travelling without a ticket. And one of his greatest pleasures these days is when he takes the younger members of his family on journeys of discovery for them and journeys of sheer nostalgia for himself, to see some of his old tramcars in the Transport Museum in Witham Street.

Visiting the Transport Museum in Witham Street and back on board tram no. 357, Harry adopts a pose which will be familiar to all those thousands of passengers who once offered him their fares on journeys to and from Castle Junction.

Willie Grey

Half Asleep in the Frying Pan

I first met Willie Grey in the summer of 1989 when I was down in Fermanagh. He was introduced to me as 'a local character' who knows the Erne, Upper and Lower, like the back of his hand. At the time he was helping the National Trust to run trips on board the replica Victorian steam yacht, *Trasna*, from Crom Castle on the Upper lough.

And no better man for the job. His knowledge of the Erne dates back to 1925 when he was six years old. In the intervening years he has been professional fisherman, boatman to the pilots of the RAF Sunderlands and Catalinas which were based in the Lower lough during the Second World War, and skipper of Fermanagh's police launches for some thirty years from the mid-fifties until his retirement in 1985.

More recently I went back to Fermanagh to talk to him again, and to listen to him recounting tales of the area and its people, something he indulges in with the greatest of pleasure. On the Erne, like most places in Ireland, you can experience all four seasons in a single day. Which is why we were standing at the viewing point on the scenic route between Lisnarick and Kesh on a sharp April day, dodging the stinging sleet showers borne on the western wind, and admiring the glimpses of silver water shining up from between the islands of the lough.

'I WAS born on 14 June 1919 at Drumall, Lisnarick. Eventually there would be six of us, three boys and three girls, but I was the eldest. It was my mother that ran the farm. She had to, for my father had been blinded at the age of 13. His sister was a dressmaker, and one day she ran out to call him in with scissors in her hand. It was a bad accident and cost him his sight.'

When his parents married in 1917 Willie told me that the blind pension was only ten shillings a week. But despite that, times were not too bad on the farm.

'The big estate at Castle Archdale nearby gave the hired hands
a free house. They'd have the milk of a cow, and the bog to cut turf.
On our farm we'd maybe have had three cows and two or three
calves, and we grew all our own produce. Then there was the flock
of turkeys. We always kept one back for ourselves at Christmas
time, but I can also remember we'd have a goose sometimes.'

When prompted more about his younger days, Willie paused for
a moment and then pointed out Drumall to me, just over the estate
trees from where we were standing.

'If we drive back down the road towards Enniskillen I'll show
you where I first went to school.'

A few minutes after taking the road south from Kesh, Castle
Archdale Parish Church came into sight, and Willie directed me off
the road onto one of the entrances to the estate, and then turned me
hard left to a tiny laneway, with a gate across it, less than a hundred
yards away. There was nothing to see, just the parish churchyard
on the left, a tiny stream, a glade of trees and the old tower of the
original parish church.

'It's long since gone now of course,' he explained, 'but the wee
schoolhouse of Drumall Primary School once stood here, between

Willie Grey.

the lane and the river. And beside it the Orange hall. It was used as the church hall, and had a small gallery. Local concerts were held there as well.'

I found it hard to believe that both a school and a hall could have stood on such a small narrow piece of land.

'Believe it or not the school held about 50 pupils. There were two schoolrooms and a yard at the back. It was run by Mrs Arthur Quinn and her sister-in-law, Miss Annie Quinn, and they created a perfect atmosphere. The pupils were mixed. There was never any talk about who was Protestant and who was Catholic. We all lived as normal human beings.

'One day the teacher was taking religious instruction, and she said to ... I think it was Robbie Rolston, "How many persons is in one God?" And he said there was three. She asked another lad, Cecil Thompson, "Can you name them, Cecil?" He says, "It was Terry Herne, Mick Maguire and James McCabe." I remember that answer to this day. All three were famous characters around Lisnarick. Terry Herne was the shoemaker, Mick Maguire used to work for the Archdales of Castle Archdale and James McCabe was a noted gamekeeper. If anyone was poaching game, James was very fast on his feet and could run very hard. Them three characters were even more famous after that story got around.

'There was one old fella, he used to go for the farmers to spread turf, and he used to take three or four young fellas and give us all tuppence a day for to spread these turf. He went into Mackies in Lisnarick - it's a different lookin' place now, it was an old pub then. He went in to get an ounce of tabaccy and a box of matches goin' to the bog. He was a Mr Aiken, with a beard nearly down to his waist, a big white beard. He always took off his boots when the summer come and ran around in bare feet, like many of the boys. In Mackies there was a Mrs Johnston, a famous lady who like a lot of other women was very fond of news, and she said to him, "Good morning, Mr Aiken, isn't that a lovely morning."

'"Indeed it is, Mrs Johnston," he says.

'She says, "Are you goin' to spread turf?"

'"Indeed I am, Mrs Johnston."

'She says, "Do you think is the weather goin' to take up?"

'"Oh, indeed it is, Mrs Johnston."

'He was standin' there in his bare feet, and she then says to him, "Them's a lovely pair of boots you're wearin'."

'"Indeed they are, Ma'am", he says. "An' I've a pair of trousers to match them, but there's a hole in the arse of them."'

I would say Willie has told that story many times but, as he says, you'd never get anything like that nowadays. Another favourite anecdote relates how Harry Mackie was drawing turf from the bog with a horse and cart and a 'led' cart. This was a second cart drawn by the first one which was filled up while the horse cart was taken back for unloading.

'One of Harry's helpers caught his foot in the reins and catapulted himself head first straight into the bog. Harry usually prefaced anything he said with the words, "Well, really." His only comment as he pulled him out of the bog-hole was, "Well, really, ye've a very awkward way of gettin' off a cart."'

And a somewhat similar story concerns David McKeen, a well-known fisherman from Lough Neagh, who came to the Erne to teach people how to fish.

'One day David was out with a fella' called Jim Robinson. It was in the wintertime and it was very cold. In fact there was snow lying in the boat. Jim asked David two questions in quick succession: "Is that water deep, and is the water cold?" And before he could get an answer Jim's foot slipped in the snow and in he went head first. When he surfaced a second or two later, David looked down at him and remarked, "I suppose that answers both questions!"'

Willie worked for the law for thirty years, but his first encounter with it happened while he was still at school, or should have been. His love of fishing, already established by the age of six, meant that at times schooling took second place to it. And there was a good livelihood to be made from it. But the law caught up with him when his mother was summonsed for his non-attendance at school. Her appearance at Irvinestown court-house was newsworthy in that the Resident Magistrate, Major Dickey, on questioning her about the valuable earnings Willie was making discovered that the pay was better than that of an R.M.!

In 1937 Willie decided to leave home and joined the Royal Inniskilling Fusiliers, but this turned out to be one of the shortest military careers on record. His father died that year and his mother had him returned to civvy street after only three and half months. He took up fishing once again, but by 1943 this was a much more precarious occupation. In any case, life on Lower Lough Erne was very different in wartime days. Castle Archdale became a major RAF installation, providing unrivalled facilities as a sea-plane base.

'Lough Erne was the best freshwater base in the world, I'd say. There was no tidal water, no salt water and it was well sheltered for all the planes. Moorings were laid between Tom's island and White island, and between the mainland and the back of White island. They had plenty of water, and lines of buoys running north-

RAF Catalinas in their secure anchorage in the lower Lough.

south and east-west marked out the landing and take off paths across the lough.'

By 1943 Willie was working for the RAF, a 'lough' pilot from Fermanagh assisting RAF pilots from wherever, taking them to and from their moorings, and guiding and escorting their Sunderlands and Catalinas between the islands. There were times when planes ran aground or even sank at their moorings. Helping with salvage work was part of the routine. But earlier, in 1941, Willie and his friend Tommy Maguire witnessed an incident which still has significance to this day.

'We were fishing one morning below the Heron island when we saw this Sunderland flying around. She flew round several times and for some unknown reason she didn't land. All of a sudden the two of us heard this unmerciful bang and we looked and we saw her crashing. Now, that plane never was lifted. She remains still in the lake. I think the reason is that there were eight or ten depth charges in her which were set to go off at a depth of 175 feet. She lies at a depth of about 165 feet which means that she's very near the depth at which they would go off. And if one went off it could set off the others.

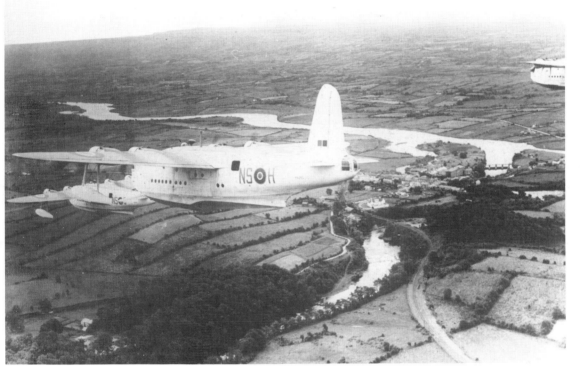

'Divers did come from Belfast to lift her but the authorities decided that she was too dangerous and so she's there to this day. The bodies of the crew were never recovered so they declared the site a war grave and nobody can interfere with her.'

In 1956 Willie joined the police and his local knowledge of the waters of the Erne served him well on the patrol launches which operated out of Enniskillen. And there was a morbid side to this work, often dealing with the results of drowning accidents. So skilled was he at recovering the victims that one of his colleagues called him 'Smell the Dead'.

But not all recovery operations were so tragic and some had their humorous side.

RAF Sunderlands returning to base in Lower Lough Erne, overflying County Donegal. The famous Belleek pottery is clearly visible.

Fermanagh folk became used to low flying aircraft during the war!

'A young fella lost his outboard engine overboard. And despite some argument about where it had been lost, I eventually found it. I had with me Inspector Norman Walmsley, and while I grappled with the engine and tried to haul it on board I got him to back the boat with the oars. But there was a bit of a breeze blowing up and Inspector Walmsley wasn't much use as an oarsman. He was futterin' about and there was some bad language on my behalf, which I must admit was not unusual.

'I must have given him some abuse because when we'd recovered the engine I turned to him and said, "Sir, we can head back to shore now."

'"Thanks very much," says he, "for giving me my rank back."

'And another time when he dropped the aerial of a radio over the side I found him staring at the spot where it had sunk. "You'll not gain much from that, Sir," says I, "for it'll not jump back up at you."'

Others too found that Willie Grey spoke his mind without regard for rank or position. For many years the police launch based at Enniskillen was called the *Muriel K*. Eventually the time came for

Constable Grey on patrol on board the police launch 'Muriel K' on the Erne.

her to be replaced because the bottom of her hull was rotting away. A surveyor from the Department of Trade came to Enniskillen to give his expert opinion. Willie met him at Castle Archdale and from a distance the surveyor commented on how well the launch looked.

'Aye,' said Willie, 'but the whole arse has fell out of her.' The official reply from the Department's representative was, 'In our profession, Mr Grey, we prefer to call it the keel!'

That episode was captured in a cartoon which appeared later in police circles showing a civil service figure in dark jacket and pinstripes standing beside a policeman in uniform, complete with baggy trousers and a revolver hanging down as if he were Wild Bill Hickock!

The *Muriel K* was replaced by a new launch which was named the *Lady Grey*, in honour of the wife of the then-Governor of Northern Ireland, Lord Grey of Naunton. On the day she was launched another outspoken police character, Superintendent Ken Cordner, ordered 26 bottles of champagne which were kept cool on ice in a large bath pan in the boat.

'Later on they were transferred to tables set out on the pontoon at Ely Lodge. I was carrying two bottles, one in each hand, and talking to Lady Grey at the same time. The superintendent called out to me, "Grey, can you not bring more bottles than two?" To which I replied, "Yes, sir, but it would look very undignified to carry them in your arms, like turf!"

'The new launch had a chrome and steel ladder on the transom, and I was surprised later on when Superintendent Cordner asked me, "Where does that ladder go, Grey?" To which I replied, "Go down it and you'll find out." But someone else said, "If you fall in, it's to pull you out." And I added, "Who the hell would want to pull you out!" He muttered, "Ask a silly question", but Lady Grey was greatly amused and gave me one of the bottles of champagne to keep for a special occasion. It did very nicely when my grand-daughter was christened.

'The name of the new launch came up again one day when some trainees were being asked some general knowledge questions by one of the training inspectors. He asked a young lady trainee, "Where is the police boat kept?"

'"At the back of the station."

'"What's its name?"

'"The *Lady Grey*."

'"Well done. And who's it named after?"

'"The wife of the man who drives her!"

'And someone once actually asked me if she was named after me.

The replacement for the 'Muriel K' was the 'Lady Grey', built for speed, and named after the wife of a former Governor of Northern Ireland.

'I said, "Lady Grey? I never knew that I'd changed my sex!"
Maybe tact was never my strong point.' But Willie Grey's
seamanship was always recognised. District Inspector Nicky
McGill once commented, 'Grey? Hmm, every hand a stilson, every
finger a marline-spike.'

Today tourism is Fermanagh's growth industry, yet prior to the
Second World War tourists were few and far between. Pre-war, apart
from local fishermen and the odd sand-yacht, the only boats
you'd have seen on the lough would have been the Fairy-class
yachts owned by the gentry. And many of those who worked on the
big estates became expert at handling and racing the Fairies.

'One of those old sand-boats, the *Wideawake* - I called her 'half-
asleep' because she only did three knots - sank near the West
Bridge. She was refloated and taken to the 'Fryin' Pan' - that's a
small inlet near Portora.'

Generally speaking the Erne provides good and safe waters for
the thousands who holiday there nowadays. Mixing with the
accents of the Province are now to be heard the foreign accents of
Germany, France, Holland, Italy and many other parts of the world.

'I always advised people who came here to boat on the lower lake
that if the weather wasn't suitable they should head for the upper
lake. Head up through Enniskillen up to Lisnaskea direction, up by
Crom, and if the weather changed for the better to head for the
lower lake.

'If you are out in the lower lake and the weather turns bad you'll
get bigger waves close in near the shore. There was a famous man,
Christy McPike, who used to say if the first big wave didn't get you,
the second would give you a bit of a shakin', and the third would
tumble you over. If you watch the waves you'll always get twelve
small waves and three big ones, but you have a short crabbit wave
in Lough Erne. Even so all the cabin cruisers on the Erne are well
built, seaworthy boats. I have never known a boat to sink yet.'

It was in 1958, obviously in anticipation of the tourist potential
of the area, that the Lough Erne Drainage people got local
fishermen to mark out the lake showing any hazards such as
shallow areas.

'I myself worked with the Erne Drainage from 1956 to 1958
putting out the markers to show where it was safe to operate. The
first markers were red and green - red for danger and green
showing the safe side. Later those colours were changed to red and
white because in the evening, when the light fades, red and green
can look the same.

'There's an old saying here that you'll see it as far as you'll see a white cow in a bog. If you keep to the white side of the mark you can't go wrong, there's no tidal waters, and it's perfectly safe. If it's blowing hard there's plenty of islands to shelter behind, or if you keep well out you'll miss the biggest waves, like the ones you find close in to the shore.'

The level of water in the lakes has been altered from time to time. As far back as 1836 the authorities drained the system and lowered the level by between 7 and 8 feet. At this time a channel was bored and blasted between Portora Castle and Enniskillen.

Willie likes to make the point that this was before his time, but can remember the next occasion when levels were adjusted.

'The Lough Erne Drainage lowered the level again in 1956, and this is now the statutory level. These days the Ballyshannon Hydro-electric Scheme can make adjustments of up to four feet, 2 feet above or below the statutory level. It's not only boating people who are affected by alterations to the water level. Pike spawn in the rushes and when the water goes down they can be left high and dry.'

Ask Willie about the names of some of the islands, and he'll list them for you in his rich Fermanagh accent, even if he couldn't tell you how they got the names.

There's Crevinishaughy, Innishmakill, Cleenishmeen, Cleenish-garve, Namanfin – which the local people call the Isle of Man – Inish Conra – known locally as Innishconnery – and over on the other side there's Maho mountain poppin' up into the sky. I was showin' some English ladies round the lake one day and giving them all the names. When I came to Owl island one of them says to me, "Oh, you Irish, you don't talk right. It's 'old' not 'oul'." I soon put her right!'

On White Island there are the remains of a small twelfth-century church and a set of carved human figures which Willie calls the stone Fermanagh men.

'They were scattered all over the place before the war. Two of them were even used as mascots beside the anti-aircraft gun emplacements on the island during the war. Two had been lying at the entrance to the castle garden at Castle Archdale.

'Then Tom McCubbin and Captain Gale gathered them up and built them into a wall. Later Jack Armstrong was out ferreting rabbits when he found the big one. It was lying face down and he dug it out with an ash pole. I call it the Bishop because the figure on it has a crook and a bell.'

If some people have on occasions been on the receiving end of Willie Grey's acerbic tongue, there's no doubt to my mind that his rich and colourful language has been enjoyed by many many more, especially those on the sidelines.

The replica Victorian steam yacht 'Trasna' which for a
time ran National Trust cruises from Crom Castle on
Upper Lough Erne.

In 1984, just before his retirement, the Dowager Duchess of Westminster, Lady Grosvenor, presented him with his British Empire Medal at Hillsborough. Others present on that formal occasion had cause to wonder about the animated and entertaining conversation which took place as the presentation was being made. Willie Grey prefers it to remain a secret.